5014

D0387665

Every Good Thing

Marilyn Morgan Helleberg

Every Good Thing

Claiming God's Gifts for You

Guideposts®
Carmel, New York 10512

Every Good Thing

To the Holy Spirit
on whose wings this book must fly
if it is to serve

Contents

Preface

There's a lake in the little valley behind our house that's a lovely sight. In the summer, canoes and sometimes a sailboat or two can be seen gliding lazily along its usually calm waters. In winter, skaters often crisscross the ice-covered surface in easy, graceful patterns. Every year in March or early April, seagulls appear from out of nowhere, and spend a couple of weeks feasting on easy-to-catch fish from the almost dry lake bed and gracing our lives with the beauty of their long, sweeping flights and haunting calls.

Some time ago, I talked with some people who had moved to Kearney from another state and bought a house in our area during a time when the canal gates were closed, so the lake was dry. Imagine their enchantment when they woke up one morning and looked out over the valley to see the lake filled! "We didn't even know there *was* a lake there!" they said. "And to think! The waters were there all the time, just waiting to be let in!"

Waters from Kearney canal irrigate area farmlands, and there's even a dam and a waterfall by which electric power is generated—all of this in addition to the beauty, the grace, and the splendor of the lake, the canoes and boats, skaters, and birds. "How rich we are to have all of this, and we didn't even know it," said the newcomers.

I am beginning to see that it's the same way with God's grace and all of the precious gifts that flow from it. His gifts are like waters that have always been there, waiting only for you and me to let them in. I invite you to join me in learning to let in more and more of God's gifts.

Don't misunderstand. I'm not telling you that reading this book will immediately bring you all of your desires. The waters of God's grace are inexhaustible, and you and I will always need to keep growing in our ability to open the gates of our lives and to expand the size of our lake beds. But I pray that you will find in the following pages some keys that will help you to open more fully to God, so that your life may become more and more grace-filled. My prayer for you is a vision, held in my heart, of a filling lake, a lake of exquisite beauty and infinite possibility. It represents your life, transformed by grace.

Acknowledgments

Before I start to write, I usually prepare an outline for each chapter, but once I begin the actual writing, I seem to work best if I just go with what comes. Often this means that I ignore the outline that was so well organized in favor of the creative touch of the moment. Can you imagine how much patience that requires from an editor who wants readers to be able to see the logical sequence of ideas so they can follow what I write? Thank God for patient editors like Mary Ruth Howes. I need her! Thanks, also, to Guideposts book editor Harold Van't Hof for inviting me back for a second book; to senior book editor Terri Castillo, who did not work directly with me in this project, but whose friendship has meant more to me this year than I can say; and to Betty Gold, the promotion people, and all the other behind-the-scenes people without whom this book could not have happened.

I also want to thank my family for their love and encouragement during the time of my writing, and my friends, especially Jan and Eugene Ward, for the touch of their lives on mine—a grace beyond measure.

Because of the personal nature of the material in the following pages, I have changed *some* names and, in a few places, minor details in order to protect the identity and feelings of the people involved. The incidents, however, are all based on true happenings and, I hope, speak of truth greater than the particulars surrounding them.

Every Good Thing

CHAPTER 1

The Gift of God's Grace

But unto every one of us is given grace according to the measure of the gift of Christ.

Ephesians 4:7

Near the end of her life, my mother removed her beautiful marquis-cut diamond ring from her finger and put it on mine. I protested and tried to give it back. "No," she said. "I want to see it on your hand. It will remind you of my love for you. I had that in mind when your father asked me to pick it out. So you see, it's *already yours* and always has been!"

At the time, it made me sad to accept Mother's ring, knowing that she was giving it to me because she knew that death was near. Besides, I certainly hadn't done anything to deserve such a valuable gift. But Mother insisted, and in the end, I accepted it. I wore it until she died a few weeks later . . . and then I put the ring away in our basement safe. I couldn't take a chance on losing it! Besides, we're just plain, middle-class people, and it seemed to me that the ring was too extravagant for me.

Mother has been gone for eleven years now. Except for a few special occasions, her gift to me has been in the safe most of the time during those years. But recently, when our extended family got together for Thanksgiving, my Aunt Connie said, "Whatever happened to your mother's beautiful ring?"

When I told my aunt it was in the safe, she said, "Oh, but I know your mother meant for you to *enjoy* her ring!"

After our company left, I got to thinking about my aunt's remark. Of course, she was right! Hadn't Mother said that she wanted the ring to be a reminder to me of her love? How could I have put it away in a dark place?

The next morning, I got the ring out and discovered anew how beautiful it was. I held it up to the light and allowed myself to enjoy its great beauty, as glints of green, blue, and silver radiated from its many facets. I still felt undeserving of it, but that was no longer the point. The simple point was that Mother gave it to me because she loved me, and because it gave *her* pleasure to give!

Grace Is Already Ours

Mother's giving me her ring has been a picture for me of God's gift to us of His grace. We can't possibly earn or deserve that. He gives it to us because, in spite of all our failings, this tenderhearted God of ours simply can't help loving us! He tells us that (like my mother's ring) His grace is *already ours* and always has been! We are heirs to it! (See 1 Peter 3:7.) Our heavenly Father meant for us to accept and *enjoy* His grace, to recognize it in the events of each day, to let it remind us of His love for us.

That God's grace—rich, extravagant, deep and many-faceted—is *already mine* has been a waking-up realization for me. His grace was mine even before I knew it had been bought for me with the life of God's Son. It is mine even when I'm most undeserving. It is present for me in the freshness of the morning, in the rhythms of the wind and the rain, and in the surrender of my body to the bed at the end of an exhausting day. It is the invisible treasure buried in suffering, the diamond chip in the heart-stab of a friend's angry words, in the pain of a migraine headache, or in the yearning for the touch of a hand that is no longer there. God's grace saturates my world, whether I acknowledge it or not.

If I take the wings of the morning
   and dwell in the uttermost parts of the sea;
even there thy hand shall lead me,
   and thy right hand shall hold me.
If I say, "Let only darkness cover me;
   and the light about me be night,"
even the darkness is not dark to thee,
   the night is bright as the day. . . .
                                    Psalm 139:9–12, RSV

God's grace, in fact, is absolutely showered upon us by His
constantly outpouring love (Ephesians 1:7).

Pictures of Grace

Like a finely cut diamond, God's grace has many facets,
every one of them beautiful beyond words. By its very nature,
grace resists being defined. We can talk about it only in
parables or metaphors, or by viewing it from different per-
spectives, all the time realizing that each view is only a part
of the whole. God's grace is the treasure hidden in a field for
which a treasure-seeker gladly sells all possessions. It is the
pearl of great price for which the merchant is willing to give
up all other riches (Matthew 13:44–46).

God's grace is in the call of Jesus Christ at which the
disciples leave all to follow Him (Matthew 4:18–22). It is in
the beauty of the organ tones that flow through my friend
Jan, as she praises God with music. It is in the sudden solid
strength to endure that comes in the still of the night to Bill,
who is dying of cancer. It is the upside-down world of Jesus
Christ, in which poverty is wealth, weakness is strength, and
failure is victory. It is in those breathless moments when my
overturned world suddenly rights itself, and I fall, limp and
laughing, into the arms of my Creator. It is hope and comfort, compassion and mercy and forgiveness. It is all of these
things. But more than anything else, it is the flutter of white
wings, the touch of the Holy Spirit, the sometimes stunning
but more often invisible and unnoticed presence of God,
surrounding, filling, upholding, *gifting* you and me.

There is grace in the hopelessly broken relationship that
somehow finds a thread-thin hope on which to rebuild itself.

There is grace in the voice that stands outside the tomb of your despair, calling you back to life. For me, there is grace in my periodic fall from self-sufficiency that makes me aware, again, of my need for other people.

Grace Experienced

Grace is rather like music in that it can't be adequately described. It can only be *experienced.* Jonathan Ford, now rector of my home church in Kearney, discovered the radical and overwhelming nature of grace while he was a seminary student. One morning, a week after carrying a heavy metal filing cabinet up a flight of stairs, he bent over the sink to shave and couldn't stand up. After two months of unceasing pain and outpatient treatment, he was hospitalized for the next twenty-four days, where he was subjected to further painful diagnostic procedures and treatments. Two and a half weeks later, his condition virtually unimproved, the young seminarian was discouraged and on the edge of despair when the chaplain from the seminary came in to pray with him, using a prayer from the 1928 *Book of Common Prayer:*

> *The Almighty Lord, who is a most strong tower to all those who put their trust in him, to whom all things in heaven, in earth, and under the earth, do bow and obey; Be now and evermore thy defence; and make thee know and feel, that there is none other Name under heaven given to man, in whom, and through whom, thou mayest receive health and salvation, but only the Name of our Lord Jesus Christ. Amen.*[1]

As the chaplain prayed those words for him, young Ford became aware that he'd been trying to get well all on his own, that he hadn't truly asked Jesus Christ to heal him. He read the prayer over so many times that he memorized it, and he began to sense a turning within himself. Five days later, he went home from the hospital in a body cast.

At the time, Ford's wife, Elaine, was working the 3:00 to 11:30 P.M. shift on the psychiatric unit of Alexandria Hospital. They had two small children, ages five and six and a half.

It soon became clear that the young father was just not physically able to handle the children and the household three days a week, and Elaine was becoming more and more exhausted. Something had to be done.

As Jack Ford dialed the number of Bishop Harry Lee Doll, he swallowed hard. It was the first time in his adult life that he had ever asked for help. Why should the bishop consider helping him, anyway? His grades were only average, and he was already receiving more financial aid than any student had ever received from the diocese of Maryland. It was the hardest phone call he'd ever had to make, but he had no choice. After explaining his predicament, Ford asked if there might be any way that Elaine could work only two days a week until he was out of the cast.

There was silence on the line. Then the bishop asked, "How much would it take for Elaine not to work *at all,* between now and September?"

Ford, wondering at the question, quickly figured in his head the amount of money Elaine would make in those nine months.

There was another fifteen-second pause, and then the bishop said, "Will it be all right if we send it to you in two checks?"

Undeserved, unearned blessing. *Grace.* And a young man whose life was changed because of it. Jonathan Ford, mediocre student, became an A scholar "because" he said, "I had experienced the gift of God's grace." Grace experienced became a transforming power.

Everything We Need

When I looked up the Scripture passages that tell about God's grace, I began to see that every truly worthwhile thing I've ever wanted is a gift of grace.

First of all, grace is the energy that activates my faith! Most Christians are familiar with the various gifts of the Spirit that Paul lists in his first letter to the church at Corinth: wisdom, knowledge, faith, healing, working of miracles, prophecy, discerning of spirits, diversities of tongues, and interpretation of tongues. These are commonly known as the charismatic gifts. But did you know that the words *charis-*

mata (meaning gifts) and *charismatic* (used to describe those gifts) are both derived from the Greek word *charis,* which means *grace?*[2] In addition to the spiritual gifts enumerated there, the Bible also makes it clear that many other blessings are ours for the claiming, including some you may not have thought of as graces, such as: wisdom and perception, the ability to reach out to others, power, comfort and hope, strength, humility, growth, sufficiency, cheer and respite, and, of course, love and forgiveness. On a grander scale, it is only by grace that we are justified, made righteous, and given eternal life. (In Appendix One, you'll find Scripture references for each of the above-named gifts.)

Clearing Away the Obstacles

Why, then, are we so unhappy? Why do we so often feel deprived, rejected, lost? Why isn't life more fulfilling? I believe the answer lies in the fact that, just as I had trouble accepting and living with Mother's ring, many of us have never learned to fully accept God's freely given grace. We're too proud, or we feel unworthy, or the gift seems too extravagant, or we're afraid of losing control, or it doesn't seem logical enough, or our expectations are too rigid, or . . . for any number of other reasons we wall ourselves off from His grace. But the exciting truth is that we *can* learn to expect, accept, and embrace His grace. Only when we're able to do that can we truly claim any of His other gifts, because *every good gift comes from and depends on God's grace.*

Even though we can't earn His grace, there is still something we can do. We can eliminate the obstacles that stand in the way of our *acceptance* of it! We can stop resisting. We can allow ourselves to be poured out in order to become empty cups, ready to be filled. This is not always easy, but doing it can transform our lives. It was only because a young woman named Mary was receptive enough to say to the angel, "Be it done unto me," that she was capable of becoming the mother of our Lord. It is only by increasing our receptivity to God the Holy Spirit that you and I may become capable of receiving the unimaginable grace of the indwelling Christ. But in order to do that, we need first to clear away the obstacles that block our receptivity.

The Obstacle of Pride

Have you ever received a gift that was very expensive, or represented hours of the giver's work, or was so creative and unusual that your gift to the other looked shabby in comparison? How did it make you feel? Unworthy, of course. How hard it is to accept a gift that you know you can never repay! The reason it's so hard is that it knocks our pride off center stage. Too often we want to be the more generous one, because that puts us one up, makes us feel good about ourselves, or gives us the edge in the relationship.

There's a similar element of pride in our inability to accept God's grace in our lives. What could I ever give God that would *begin* to come close to the gift of His grace to me? Obviously, there is nothing, absolutely nothing; because everything I have—even my very life—comes from Him and is already His. So accepting God's grace requires a certain element of humility. I need to be able to admit to myself and to God that I have *nothing* to give in return. Maybe that's what Jesus meant when He said, "Blessed are the poor in spirit: for theirs is the kingdom of heaven" (Matthew 5:3). Oh, yes! Poverty of spirit means I have nothing to give and I know it!

Once the awareness of our poverty becomes real, we can let go of our pride and just allow God to be the giver. Doing that will open up new channels through which His grace may flow into our lives!

Several years ago, I came across a prayer by a sixteenth-century saint named Ignatius. The prayer symbolizes for me true poverty of spirit. It came to me at a time when I was just beginning a work project, so I felt a special need to empty myself in order that God's will might be done in my work. When I first started using the prayer, it seemed that I was giving up something to God, but as I continued to pray it every day, I began to see that, in truth, *He* was gifting *me.* My life and my work began to be filled with blessings beyond measure.

After the project was successfully finished, I'm ashamed to admit, I slipped out of the habit of praying that prayer. (I seem to do that often—enjoy the fruits of God's grace and then let the spiritual gift slip through my fingers out of neglect!) So, I've resolved to start praying St. Ignatius' prayer again every day.

Take, Lord, receive
all my liberty, my memory, my understanding,
my entire will.
Give me only Your love and Your grace.

Take, Lord, receive
all I have and possess.
You have given all to me; now I return it.
Give me only Your love and Your grace.

Take, Lord, receive.
All is Yours now.
Dispose of it wholly according to Your will.
Give me only Your love and Your grace.

Amen.

The Obstacle of Unworthiness

Strangely enough, pride and feelings of unworthiness sometimes go hand-in-glove. They are cut into the grooves on opposite sides of the same record. Feeling unworthy sometimes masks itself as being humble, but there's a vast difference between humility (lack of false pride) and low self-esteem. Humility says, "Without God, I am nothing." Low self-esteem says, "I'm just no good." The difference, of course, is reliance on God versus estrangement from Him.

Most feelings of unworthiness begin in childhood. I know a young man whose father repeatedly said to him, "You're no good. You're a bum. You're lazy. You're never going to amount to anything." Of course, the child accepted his father's evaluation. Despite the fact that he's very intelligent, Peter (name changed) dropped out of school in the eleventh grade. He married young and had several children right away. There has been serious trouble in his marriage, and Peter has had a difficult time finding work and keeping a good job. It's very hard for him to see God as a loving Father, because his human father was so critical and rejecting of him.

Recently, though, with the help of a counselor, this father

and son have been working through some of their old conflict. It has become clear to them that the father was treated
in exactly the same way by *his* father, and there is some
evidence that the pattern was there even in the generation
before that. What a destructive chain! Peter is absolutely
determined that he will break the chain, and I believe that,
with God's help and *by His grace,* he will do just that.
Already, Peter is a loving father who holds his children,
plays with them, and encourages them instead of criticizing.

How often, like this young father, we miss the gift of God's
grace because of feelings of unworthiness generated by past
experiences. We need to learn to say to ourselves, "Yes, I am
unworthy of God's gifts, but He doesn't ask worthiness of
me. He accepts me just as I am. There is something infinitely
beautiful and lovely within me because I am God's child. I
am so precious to God that He gave His Son for me. I'll
accept and claim that loveliness in myself. I can do that
because Christ made it possible!"

The Obstacle of Our Real Guilt

Of course, low self-esteem is not the same thing as the
problem of our *very real guilt,* our own sinfulness, that separates us from God. A recent experience forcefully illustrated
for me the separating power of sin. One day I heard a rumor
about someone I already had negative feelings about. Before
the day was over, I had passed that gossip on to three other
people! That evening when I sat down for my evening prayer
time, I had a great deal of trouble focusing on God, because
the rumor kept coming into my mind. Then I realized that
God was trying to show me my error. Of course! "Never
repeat what you are told and you will come to no harm;
whether to friend or foe, do not talk about it, unless it would
be sinful not to, do not reveal it" (Ecclesiasticus 19:8, JB).

Although I confessed my sin to God, I still felt guilty
about it, and I continued to have trouble focusing on prayer.
The next evening, the Scripture reading was Romans 5.
When I came to verse 20, I was stunned. Paul writes that
"where sin abounded, grace did much more abound" (Romans 5:20). The Greek word here translated as *abound*
means *increase!* Incredible! Where there is great sin, there is

even greater grace! The greater my sin, the more His grace increases!

Now of course this doesn't mean that I should deliberately sin in order to obtain grace. It doesn't work that way at all. But it does mean that *my heavenly Father's grace is always greater than my sinfulness.* Always. "Sin shall not have dominion over you: for ye are not under the law, but under grace" (Romans 6:14).

Once aware of that precious fact, I was able to go to the woman in question and apologize for talking about her. She assured me the rumor wasn't true, so I corrected it with those I'd told. My reason for telling you this is that I know I could never have done that by myself. It's very hard for me to face people I've wronged and admit my error. It was made possible only because of God's abounding grace that is always greater than my sin.

Sin is estrangement from God, but grace, which is infusion of love, *overcomes estrangement* . . . because of Jesus Christ!

I like what Matthew Fox says about forgiveness.

> Forgiveness is another word for letting go. We are saved by forgiveness, the power to forgive ourselves, to allow ourselves to be forgiven, which matures into the power to forgive others and allow them their time to be forgiven. Forgiveness is about letting go of guilt—some imagined, some real—and about letting go of fear. There is no healing, no salvation, without forgiveness. And with forgiveness all things become saved and healed once again. Creation is restored.[3]

In chapter 2, we'll look at some ways to let go of our guilt so that we can accept the grace of God's total forgiveness.

The Obstacle of Feelings

It's very important to realize that God's grace is not dependent upon the way we *feel.* Our heavenly Father loves us, whether we feel it or not, and He has demonstrated His love and grace decisively throughout the history of the world. I think of that forty-year journey of God's people through the desert as they traveled away from their bondage in Egypt. Oh, the grumbling that went on! Many times they felt completely deserted by God. Again and again they complained to Moses that they should never have come—they were better off as slaves in Egypt than starving in the desert! Yet God's grace was with them, every step of the barren way, and He demonstrated it time and again—by parting the Red Sea, sending manna and quail for food, having water gush from a rock, saving the Israelites from the Amalekites and other enemies, and in many other ways.

Even when we feel most unloved, His love and grace are still ours. It is impossible that God's grace was ever *not* with His Son. Yet Jesus cried out on the cross, "My God, my God, why hast thou forsaken me?" If I can remind myself of that when I'm feeling unloved or rejected for any reason, I can *will to believe* that God's love and grace are with me. Sometimes, then, the feeling follows. When it does, I can rejoice and give thanks. (The feeling doesn't make the grace any more real; it just helps me to know it's there.) But even when the emotion doesn't follow, you and I can continue to affirm the presence of God's love and grace.

Sometimes it's only in looking back that we can see the subtle but sure movements of the Holy Spirit in our lives. So, feeling the grace of God is a great blessing, something to be hoped for and to cherish when it happens, and it definitely can be evidence of His grace. But the absence of that feeling does not mean that grace is absent from us.

The Obstacle of Limiting Thought Patterns

Another thing that sometimes interferes with our ability to receive God's grace is the need that many of us have to make everything fit into a logical, rational pattern. Sometimes I need to be reminded of what John the Baptist told his followers about his cousin, Jesus: "the law was given by Moses, but grace and truth came by Jesus Christ" (John 1:17).

I have a friend who is studying to become a minister. He told me that, after several days of reading pro and con arguments about different aspects of theology, his head was reeling and it all seemed meaningless. So he gave up on his studying, went into the sanctuary of the church, and played a tape of some beautiful classical music. As he let go of all of the thoughts that were swarming around in his mind, he felt the presence of God in a fresh, new way, and all the internal contradictions came together in a new kind of harmonious unity. Grace!

I suppose that grace may sometimes come while our minds are busy figuring things out, but I'm convinced that we're much more likely to sense the gentle brush of its presence once we've cleared our minds of all the linear thought processes and just shifted into the intuitive, creative part of our mind that senses beauty and sees things whole, rather than fragmented. I don't believe that we can make God's grace fit into a logical, linear way of thinking. It defies definition precisely because it is "God Himself, His loving energy at work!"[4] So listening to beautiful music, reading poetry, spending time outside soaking up nature's beauty—whatever we can do that will put us in a receptive, imaginative, creative state of mind—will make us more open to His grace. Being human, we'll always be placing obstacles in the way of God's grace in our lives, but as long as we're aware of that and trying to let go of those deterrents, God will help us to move beyond them to acceptance.

Accepting the Gift

As I see it, claiming God's gifts is a two-part process, beginning with *receptivity to grace,* and followed by an *active acceptance and use* of the gifts that can transform our lives. Have you ever noticed that a healthy plant turns its leaves toward the sun, exposing as much surface as possible? That way it can receive the maximum amount of warmth and light. Once it has absorbed the sunlight, it enters into a more active phase of transforming what it has received into life-sustaining, greening chlorophyll. In the same way, you and I need to expose ourselves as fully as we can to the warmth and light of God's grace, which means becoming fully alert to its shining presence. Once we're truly open to grace, we can then actively seek, accept, and put to use the gifts God offers us. For example, in chapter 4 we'll be looking at the gift of intimacy with God. Now, there are some very specific things we can do that will help us develop such an intimate relationship, but they won't work at all unless we are open and receptive to God, unless we already know that, as Jesus said, the one "who abides in me, and I in him, he it is that bears much fruit, for apart from me you can do nothing" (John 15:5, RSV). That's grace. That's pure gift.

Another example: We cannot accept and use the gift of realness (which means being honest with ourselves, with God, and with other people) unless we've learned to trust that God is truly a loving Father who really wants to give us every good thing. I believe that the only way we can know that is by being deeply receptive to His grace.

It's the same with all the other gifts we'll be looking at. As we become more and more *aware* of the gentle dance of God's grace in our lives, we can begin to develop what I call a fresh-start attitude. We'll gain flexibility so that our ideas can expand and we can shake off old habits that have been enslaving us. We'll come to know what our real treasures are, both material and spiritual. With God's grace to guide us, we'll learn to steer our way through life with gentleness and a peaceful spirit. Finally, as we continue to open ourselves more and more to God's grace, our ability to truly serve Him and our fellow human beings will be multiplied, because God will perform that which is appointed for us (see Job 23:14).

The Way of Nonresistance

God's grace is always a birthing, a creative act, and we human beings are sometimes privileged to be the instruments of the Creator's grace. We cannot make this happen. All we can do is to be available and allow ourselves *the joy of nonresistance.* It is not unlike giving birth to a child.

When my first child was born, I was very fearful because I'd heard such horror stories about the pain of childbirth that I tensed up and fought each contraction. Of course, this only prolonged the labor and increased my pain. By the time our second child was ready to be born, I'd read a book about natural childbirth and had practiced the relaxation and breathing exercises long before labor started. I knew that the best way I could assist with the delivery was to relax and just *go with* what was happening. It was a far easier birth!

I need to remember that grace can come to me in the midst of pain (and it often does). I need to keep reminding myself when I feel most out of control, or when my carefully de-signed plans get all tangled up, that if I can just relax and go with it, offer it all to God and let go of my resistance, at the very moment of "going under," grace may descend on me like a dove.

Receptivity. That's the key. I need to become a cup, a vase, an empty vessel. "Everything that is to be receptive must and ought to be empty," observed Meister Eckhart.[5] A truly emptied person is so vulnerable to beauty and truth, so full of compassion and empathy, that he or she can become a wonderfully clear channel for God's grace. Jesus emptied Himself continually, letting go of any temptation toward pride or power, allowing Himself to be truly open so that His Father's grace could flow with great intensity and sensitivity and healing force into the world and into individual people. "Truly, truly, I say to you, the Son can do nothing of his own accord, but only what he sees the Father doing" (John 5:19, RSV). We, too, are invited to pattern ourselves after our divine yet human, emptied-vessel God.

There was a time when the idea of letting go, of emptying myself, stirred up feelings of anxiety in me. Maybe you have some of those feelings, too. But the marvelous paradox is that in the emptiness we discover the only fullness that lasts. Only in letting go can we know the strength and realness of the Father's arms.

I am not talking about asceticism (deliberately depriving yourself of real needs), or about austerity (living under harsh or severe circumstances). I *am* talking about the overwhelm-ing grace that comes when you have let go of the little and big things that are separating you from God, when you have shown your willingness to offer Him anything that has become more important to you than He is. I think that is the real point of the story of Abraham and Isaac. As a child, I could not imagine a father who would be willing to sacrifice his son, or a God who would ask such a thing. Of course, God did *not* require that sacrifice. He only wanted to know that this man loved Him with his whole heart. While Abra-ham was building the fire on which to sacrifice Isaac, God provided a ram for the offering. The point is that we need to be *willing* to offer to God anything that has become more important to us than He is. We can do that, knowing that what we freely give to Him, He will return to us in greater measure than we could possibly dream.

In Catherine Marshall's book *A Closer Walk,* she points out that, at the very moment Abraham was trudging up the mountain, struggling with the pain of what he felt he had to do . . . at that very moment, the ram was already traveling up the *other* side of the mountain! "God always is working on the 'ram part'—the escape, God's own way out."[6] I know this is true because it has happened in my own life.

Every now and then, I tend to think I really don't need other people very much. I have my relationship with God, my family, and my work, and I honestly enjoy my "alone time." When I get into that state of mind, I begin to neglect my friendships. This was my situation several months ago, when many unexpected difficulties came into my life. I began to feel very lonely, and I was suddenly aware that all of my feelings of not needing other people were false. I *do* need others. But somehow, in my state of mind at the time, I couldn't seem to reach out. All I could do was to come, empty, before God, offering Him my need.

On the day when my personal problems seemed most overwhelming, I received a phone call from our new minister's wife, who was feeling depressed because she'd had to leave all of her close friends and her work to move to Kearney. Jan and I started spending time together, and our friendship blossomed in a glorious way. She is just the kind of friend I've always hoped for, and she says the same about me. We both agree that only God could have arranged it and timed it so perfectly. And to think: during the time when we both felt most hopeless, God was already leading her up one side of the mountain and me up the other. By His grace, we were both empty enough to receive His gift.

Even though there are unsettling changes taking place in my life right now, I can let go. I don't have to cling. I can know that on the other side of the mountain and moving toward me at this moment is God's ram, the fulfillment I long for. When we're at the bottom of the pit and we're sure that life couldn't get any worse, at that very moment God is preparing the resolution to our problem.

The Secret of the Increase

Phillips Brooks wrote, "There is no such way to attain a greater measure of grace as for a man to live up to the little grace he has."[7] You and I can begin, in whatever way is open to us at this second, to let God's grace flow out from us. Even as we pray for His grace to come to us, let us open up a way to let it flow from us. There is a law of circulation in the universe: inflow increases in proportion to outflow.

Here is a prayer for the start of each day that will help prepare an opening for God's grace to enter in:

> *Heavenly Father, I thank You for the gift of this day. Even though there is nothing I could give You that would compare with it, I accept Your gift and offer it back for Your use. As its minutes and hours unfold, help me to be an empty cup. Fill me with Your grace—then help me to pour it out for others. In Jesus' name.* Amen.

NOTES

1. *The Book of Common Prayer* (New York: Oxford University Press, 1928), p. 314.

2. I am indebted to my editor, Mary Ruth Howes, for bringing this to my attention.

3. Matthew Fox, *Original Blessing* (Santa Fe, N.M.: Bear & Company, 1983), p. 163.

4. Evelyn Underhill, cited in Carroll E. Simcox, *A Treasury of Quotations on Christian Themes* (New York: Seabury Press, 1975), pp. 134–135.

5. Meister Eckhart, cited by Fox in *Original Blessing,* p. 159.

6. Catherine Marshall, *A Closer Walk* (Old Tappan, N.J.: Chosen Books, 1986), pp. 188–189.

7. Phillips Brooks, cited by Simcox in *Treasury of Quotations,* p. 135.

CHAPTER 2

The Gift of a Fresh Start

Behold, I make all things new.

Revelation 21:5

Sometime during my grade school years, I remember trying to do a watercolor painting of a mountain scene. It was not turning out the way I had envisioned it, so I kept adding more paint. The more I dabbed away at it, the muddier it became, until finally I got so frustrated I started to cry. My art teacher was a lovely, sensitive lady who very quietly and gently walked back to where I sat, put her hand on my shoulder, and asked, "May I have this painting? I'd like to keep it." When I looked up at her, nodding my head in surprise, she placed a new, clean white sheet of watercolor paper in front of me and brought me a fresh tin of water. "You'll do fine," she said. "All you need is a fresh start!"

I've thought about that many times since. If you've ever worked with watercolor, you know that there comes a point at which reworking the old stuff is not effective. If you keep trying to add color or change something, it just gets worse and worse, and you end up with a grayish-brown mess! The only way to improve the painting, then, is to let go of the old one and begin again. Give yourself a fresh start!

I think there's also such a thing as a *fresh-start attitude* that can make all the difference in the way our lives unfold. If I'm willing to let God take away the muddied-up mess I've made, He is always ready to give me a new, clean, white sheet of paper, a chance to start over, the opportunity to begin again to make things right. That gives me hope. This is one of His best gifts, truly a *grace* . . . as beautiful and delicate as butterfly wings emerging from a dull gray cocoon.

A Spiritual Revolution

There's something about new beginnings that cuts through acres of dullness, that wakes us up, that makes life worth living again. A fresh start can reawaken our sense of wonder and bring us the joy of discovery. It can revolutionize our lives.

Can you remember what spring felt like when you were five years old? Can you recall the feel of walking barefoot in the grass after a summer rain? Do you remember your first-grade reading class, with the little chairs in a circle at the front of the room, and the thrill you felt when you found out you could decipher words? Think of the new beginnings in your life—new love, marriage, new baby, new birth in Christ. God has even more new beginnings in store for us, and we can receive His gifts if we have a fresh-start attitude.

Letting Go of the Past

How do we develop a fresh-start attitude? First of all, we need to be able to let go of the past.

In every experience of change there is pain as well as gain. We need to embrace both, then let go of the pain and accept the gain. The Apostle Paul put it this way: "You must put aside your old self, which gets corrupted by following illusory desires. Your mind must be renewed by a *spiritual revolution* so that you can put on the new self that has been created in God's way, in the goodness and holiness of truth" (Ephesians 4:22–23, JB, italics mine). Paul is saying that if I try to begin again without first letting go of the past, my mind may fool me into thinking that I'm a new person, when actually the old self is just pushed down and covered over. So make no mistake—we really *are* talking about a "spiritual revolution" within, one that will give birth to our new self!

The aim of this spiritual revolution is simply to seek nothing—that's *nothing*—but God. It means that just for today, I'll put away my want list. I'll set aside my worry list. I'll try to totally let go of the past. In prayer, I'll ask for only one thing—a closer relationship with God.

There's a marvelous secret in this—the reward Jesus promised: "When you pray, go into your room and shut the door and pray to your Father who is in secret; and your Father who sees in secret will reward you" (Matthew 6:6, RSV). *How* will He reward me? What is that reward? It is nothing less than God Himself, the *withness* of Him, the combination of the Father and you, which is absolutely unbeatable.

Do you see what that means? It means that, by this spiritual revolution, you and I can be infused with *new spiritual energy,* which is the grace of God Himself. Then comes the paradox. Once we've cleared our mind and soul to the point that we want only God, we discover that *with Him comes every good thing!* The spiritual energy of grace draws to us whatever will best fulfill our deepest needs.

How can we begin to let go of the mental clutter from our past? There's only one way that has lasting effectiveness, and that's to give God all of it, both the pain and the joy, so that He can give us a fresh new start, just as my art teacher took away my muddied-up painting so I could begin again.

It's easy to see the need for letting go of our past suffering (and we'll go into that shortly). It's a little more difficult to understand our need to offer God the happy memories, too. Yet we truly need to do that.

Kiss the Flying Joy

It's natural to want to keep on savoring the precious moments we've had in the past, the joys and triumphs we've experienced. But if we begin to *live* in the past, we cheat ourselves out of the present moment.

A young friend of mine lost her husband in a car accident several years ago and, until very recently, most of her conversations centered around Hal and all the wonderful things they used to do together. She wasn't being negative, but she was living so much in the past that when a very attractive young man came along and befriended her, she almost drove him away by talking about the past. The only topic of conversation she seemed to enjoy was, "How wonderful it was to have been married to Hal." Fortunately, her new friend was able to tell her, honestly, that he wanted her always to keep her memories of Hal alive, but that it was time to get on with her life. At first Janie resented that, but gradually, through prayer, she was able to begin to let go of the past and start fresh.

Janie's experience makes me think of William Blake's slightly bittersweet but deeply moving lines,

> He who binds to himself a joy
> Does the winged life destroy;
> But he who kisses the joy as it flies
> Lives in eternity's sunrise.[1]

Instead of clutching and clinging to our joyful memories, let's kiss them and let them fly. They won't be lost! Like homing pigeons, they'll return, bringing with them gifts of *new* joys to refresh and renew our spirits and give us hope for all of our tomorrows.

Christian speaker John Claypool tells a wonderful story about a dying man named Charlie who was visited by his minister. Charlie told his friend that all of his life he'd dreaded death, but now that it was near, he realized he was already familiar with the process. Many times during his life he had let go of a little familiar world in order to have access to a greater world. For example, when he was six years old, he let go of long, lazy mornings in the sand pile and went into an unknown and threatening world called *school.* School, of course, turned out to be a place of incredible possibilities. Again and again, he had repeated this process through life, so what he was about to do was nothing new to him at all. Charlie's last words to his pastor were: "Every exit is also an entrance. You never walk out of anything without walking into something else."

A few days later, as the minister finished conducting the funeral service and walked back up the aisle in front of Charlie's casket, he felt a great heaviness, a deep sense of loss. At that moment, he looked up and saw, over the back door of the sanctuary through which Charlie's casket was at that moment passing, four red letters: E X I T. Charlie's words of a few days before came back to him—"Every exit is also an entrance"—and the thought gave him hope.[2]

I need to remember Charlie's words whenever I have to die a little death by letting go of something from my past. *Every exit is also an entrance*—and with a fresh-start attitude, it can be an entrance into a world of incredible promise.

When I think of that, the familiar passage from Romans 6:3–4 takes on new meaning: "Do you not know that all of us who have been baptized into Christ Jesus were baptized into his death? We were buried therefore with him by baptism into death, so that as Christ was raised from the dead by the glory of the Father, *we too might walk in newness of life*" (RSV, italics mine). Now is the time for walking in that newness!

Being Our Age

There is a certain sweet sadness at the end of each of life's eras, isn't there? Who has not cried at high school or college graduation, or at the wedding of a best friend, or a brother, or an only daughter? We say we are crying because we're so happy, and that's true, and yet there is more to it than that. We cry because life refuses to stand still for us. We cry because, even as we embrace the happy event, we know that we are also saying good-bye to the past. We cry because of the beauty and the fragility of human life. We cry because of our own aging.

But when you think about it, would you really want to be a teenager again, with all of those mixed-up hormones making you crazy with laughter one minute and full of tears the next? With homework every night, uncertainty about whether or not you'd have a date for the prom, and the agony of acne? One trip through that forest was enough for me! Yet at the time it was not easy to leave that teenage world behind and move toward the world of independence.

I had been so eager to go away to college. I saw it as an adventure into freedom, and I could hardly wait to try my wings. Then one September day, it happened. The last suitcase was in the trunk of my brother's car. My clothes were hanging neatly on a rod in the back seat. There was nothing left to do but to leave. Yet the four of us stood there, with forced smiles on our faces, continuing to talk about absolutely nothing. Finally, I gave Mother and Daddy each a quick hug and kiss, plopped into the passenger seat of the car, and got terribly busy fooling with the radio knobs as we drove away. I wanted nothing more at that moment than to hop out of the car, run back to my mother, and cry in her arms. But I didn't do it. I think it was in that moment that I began to let go of my childhood. I have been letting go of it ever since.

Though the times, places, and people change, all of us reenact that good-bye to childhood many times during our lives. Each time we release a part of our past, even though it may be painful to do so, we grow. That's the gift that stands waiting for us on the other side of change.

Another moment that's etched in my memory is the day John, my youngest child, started to school. I'd been looking forward to those extra hours in each day when I'd have the house all to myself. But I felt a real twinge when he got out of the car in front of the school and, without even waving good-bye, ran right into the arms of his kindergarten teacher! I could barely see as I drove home, because I knew that the door had closed on one stage of my motherhood. I went home and cried for a while, but I realized that that was okay. If there's pain in saying good-bye to our past, I think it's very important to let ourselves grieve. Only then can we truly let it go.

Of course, there were marvelous gifts to make up for my loss of being a full-time mother. I enrolled in some graduate-level classes and later taught part-time in the English Department at Kearney State College, a dream I'd given up when my first child was born. Besides that, it was very exciting to see the new relationship that developed between John and me as he grew in maturity. Instead of my reading bed-time stories to him, he often read to me. On winter afternoons, before the older children got home from school, John and I would have cocoa and cookies and talk about things that were important to him and things that mattered a lot to me. John quickly developed a strong interest in science, so we sent for a science series and did some of the experiments together. We became friends in a special way that was not possible before school opened him up to new possibilities.

Every age has its special rewards, though sometimes we can't see that until we've crossed a decade line and are looking back. When I turned thirty, I thought: I never want to be twenty again; things were too uncertain then. In my forties, I was glad I'd left behind those rather hectic thirties years. Now that I'm in my fifties, I feel sure that this is the most satisfying time of life because I'm old enough to have decided to be who I am rather than operating out of the need to please everyone else. Of course, each age also has its pain, but I have been through enough decades now to trust the gifts of the waiting years.

Transforming Past Pain

Another essential part of "putting aside our old self" is to deal with painful memories of the past, because they can keep us stuck in patterns that cause us to react to people and to circumstances in negative ways. And no matter how happy our childhood, no matter how idyllic our recent past, every one of us has some painful memories.

If your emotional pain is very deep or has stayed with you for a very long time, I urge you to seek professional help from a counselor—either a clergy person or a counseling professional. There is no shame in this. In fact, it's been my experience that people who have had counseling make wonderful friends. They are often much more sensitive to the feelings of others, more honest about their own emotions, and more comfortable about who they are. I do think it's important to look for a counselor who has a spiritual life of his or her own, because I firmly believe that therapy that centers completely on the mind and the emotions may leave a starved and shriveled spirit.

Perhaps, though, you don't need professional help to be able to release your painful past. The thing that has helped me the most in processing my old hurts has been to *re-experience them, with Jesus at my side.*

Twelve years after my father's death, I realized that I had never fully grieved the loss of him. When he died, I kept saying that it was a time for celebration, because he had gone

on to a greater life. Of course, that was true and I felt it in
my bones. But there were other emotions in me that I later
realized I'd been denying, such as the terrible emptiness that
burned at the place in my life where he had been; some guilt
I'd felt about the fact that I'd failed to call my folks the
Sunday night before (I could have talked with Daddy one
more time!); and even some anger at God for taking my dad
so suddenly at the age of seventy, with so much yet to live
for.

At a weekend retreat, a minister taught me this way of
working through my grief. First, he had me do some mild
physical exercise and deep breathing, so I could be relaxed
and open to the prayer experience that he was going to lead
me through. Then he asked me to close my eyes and go in
my imagination to a beautiful place where I'd found peace
at some time. I chose to go to the little creek that's across
the road from our cabin in the Colorado Rockies. He asked
me to look all around, in my mind's eye, noticing as many
details of my surroundings as possible, listening for the
sounds, sensing the feel and scent of the air. As I did this,
the scene really came alive in my imagination. Then he told
me to look down the road and see a man in a glistening white
robe approaching me. As He came nearer, I could see that
it was Jesus. The minister asked me to mentally reach out
and touch Jesus and then to allow myself to feel our Lord's
loving arms around me.

Next, I was to ask myself, and answer as honestly as
possible: "Am I truly ready to let go of my grief and give it
to Jesus?" (Later, I learned that this is an important question, because some people really don't want to give up their
pain. Until they actually make that decision, it will continue
to stay with them.) If I was sure I was ready, then I was to
ask Jesus to walk through my grief with me, and I was to
let the pain be pain.

I started with the phone call from my brother, telling me
of my dad's death. First, I visualized Jesus there in the
kitchen with me, and then I let myself answer the phone. As
I relived that moment, I realized that my original reaction
on that night in 1968 had been disbelief. Now, I let myself
feel the awful stab of knowing, in that moment, that my
father was truly and irrevocably dead. Instead of the wall

that I'd immediately thrown up around myself that night in 1968, I now let my pain be pain. I felt like a helpless little child again as I turned to Jesus and shouted, "No! No! Don't let this be true!" Then, my protest suddenly became anger. "How *could* God do this? How?!! It's so unfair! Bring back my daddy!"

Jesus just stood there quietly, peacefully, letting me get it all out. Then, in a moment of utter relinquishment, I fell into His arms and started sobbing. Up to this point, the experience had all been in my imagination, but now I realized that I was actually sobbing aloud. The minister put his arms around me and let me cry until all of the pain was poured out. Then he led me in a prayer of thanksgiving for the release of my long-postponed grief.

I repeated this type of visualization prayer at home several times after that, each time reliving and releasing a different aspect of my feelings about my father's death. I still miss him, of course, but I've let go of the pain of his death and started afresh with my life.

Since then, I've let go of many painful memories by reliving them in the presence of Jesus. Some of them have been deep griefs, but many have been little stings, some as small and seemingly insignificant as an embarrassing moment when I said something dumb. No matter what the pain has been, my Teacher, Jesus, has taken away the blotched page and replaced it with a clean, new, white sheet, a fresh start. And there's a delightful bonus—along with this has come the grace of a greatly increased energy level! No doubt that is because I'm no longer expending energy trying to push down the beach ball[3] of my unprocessed pain below the surface of my thoughts.

Removing Guilt

No discussion about letting go of the past could possibly omit the greatest grace of all, God's forgiveness of our sinfulness. We've all heard Jesus' story of the prodigal son so many times that there are some things that escape our notice, such as the fact that no judgment is passed on the returning son, who has wasted his inheritance in riotous living. The merciful father interrupts his son's confession, falls on his neck, has festive clothing, ring, and sandals brought, the fatted calf slaughtered, and a feast held. This is grace in its highest form! This, too, is how the servant, the moneylender, the tax collector, and the lost sheep in Jesus' stories experience generosity, forgiveness, compassion, grace. Acceptance is absolute, without special conditions, so that the person liberated can live again, can accept himself, can have a new chance in life.

Of course, repentance is necessary, a turning around, a sorrow for one's failure to act as God's beloved child should act. The prodigal son admits that he is no longer worthy to be called "son." We need to do that, too. Some find it helpful to confess their sinfulness to a clergy person. Others are able to share their failings with a trusted spiritual friend. We can also go directly to our Lord. Periodically, I set aside time to *write out* the things I'm feeling guilty about, being as honest as I possibly can. Then I lay my hands on the paper and offer it all to God in prayer, asking His forgiveness. Finally, I destroy the paper.

Then the hardest part begins—*accepting* God's forgiveness! It's so very hard not to keep running the old tapes of our guilts over and over in our minds; but that's not only a very unhealthy thing to do, it's also a denial of the gift of Jesus Christ, who died on the cross that our sins might be completely removed from us. The word *conversion* helps me know that Christ is in my turning. The literal meaning of the word is to turn around *with.* To me, the greatest mystery is that He turns around with me—again and again and again, even though I don't deserve it. Oh, yes. There it is again. Grace!

Once, when I was having a very hard time getting rid of guilt feelings about a past incident, God helped me accept His forgiveness by leading me through a symbolic cleansing. Did you know that one of the original purposes of baptism was to help human beings accept the grace of God's forgiveness (Romans 6:4ff)? In Old Testament times, ritual cleansings served this purpose. In this situation, I'd prayed for God's forgiveness and resolved to do my very best, with His help, to avoid repeating my mistake, but I still felt heavy with guilt.

As I was getting ready for bed one evening, it occurred to me to ask God to cleanse my soul and spirit as I cleansed my body. Then I took a long, refreshing shower, praying that all my guilt would be washed away. While the water ran over my body, I imagined that it was washing away all traces of my sinfulness; and when I stepped out of my bath, I affirmed that I truly *was* a new creature in Christ. It seemed to me that, like a flowing river, my heavenly Father had claimed all the debris of my life, bearing it all away, giving me the wonderful gift of a fresh start!

If you have trouble with guilt feelings that won't go away, maybe a prayer of confession followed by a ritual cleansing would help you, as it did me.

Finding the Humor in Embarrassing Moments

While we're clearing away our mental clutter, let's see what we can do about those old embarrassing moments that tend to cling to our memories and replay themselves. The one thing that's helped me here more than any other is to look for the humor in the situation. Then I can laugh at my silly pride that caused me to take myself so seriously. Well, isn't that it, really? Isn't *pride* the true reason the incident was so embarrassing? Who wants pride, anyway? It's one of the seven deadly sins! After finding the humor (which is almost always there), I can thank God for the incident because it chipped away a little bit of my false pride. I may even tell someone else about my silly (or stupid or awkward) actions and laugh with them, at myself. It's so healing. Then I can finally let God have that embarrassing moment.

For example, on the first day our new minister joined our small morning prayer group, it was my turn to lead the service. When it was time to read the psalm, I turned to Jack Ludden, who was sitting next to me in the circle, and said, "Jack, would you begin, please?" Immediately, *Father Ford* started to read the psalm. Then I realized that he thought I'd called *him* by his first name, which is also Jack! I was so embarrassed! Surely he'd think I was disrespectful!

Do you see what my embarrassment was about? My own image! As in most embarrassing situations, *pride* was the hook. All day, I kept replaying the incident in my own mind and asking myself, "What will he think of me?" Later, as I talked to another member of the prayer group, she said,

"Well, I wondered what that was all about. I thought you were getting chummy awfully fast!" Suddenly, the whole incident lost its heaviness as Cheri and I laughed about the mixup. After that, I was able to let go of it.

If there's some embarrassment, old or new, that you keep replaying, look first for the pride in it, and then for the humor. Tell it to a friend and laugh at yourself. Then give it to God and let it go.

Growing by letting go. That's what it's all about. The letting go is an ongoing process, so we don't need to have accomplished it in every phase of our lives before moving on. We just need to remember to keep releasing the past as we go along, in order to open ourselves for the gifts God is waiting to give us.

Invitation to Newness

Now that we've considered the ways we need to let go of the past, we're ready to move on to the development of a fresh-start attitude, an outlook that focuses on this moment as well as the future, a vibrant expectancy that *invites in* our God with His gift-laden arms. Our fresh start may begin, as it did for so many people in the Bible, with the gift of a new name.

Receiving a New Name

Have you noticed that, again and again in the Bible, God gives a new name to those He has chosen? Abram becomes Abraham. Jacob becomes Israel. Simon becomes Peter. Saul the persecutor of Jesus' followers becomes Paul the apostle.

It is very clear that, no matter what their past has been, God is always willing and ready to give his beloved people a fresh start. Take Jacob, for example. His name means *heel-catcher* and refers to the fact that he was born clutching his twin brother's heel. But its symbolic meaning is *one who stumbles* or *one who trips up another.* That name certainly fit this man, who was a devious trickster. We see him cheating his brother out of his birthright, deceiving his father, and taking over his uncle's best herds in a very sneaky way. When he arrived at the river Jabbok on his way back to Canaan, he feared his brother Esau's revenge, so he divided his company and sent them all ahead—even his family—while he spent the night alone on the safe side of the river.

But in the night, Jacob wrestled with "a man." After a night of struggle, Jacob said, "I will not let you go, unless you bless me." The man asked his name and then said, "Your name shall no more be called Jacob, but Israel, for you have striven with God and with men, and have prevailed" (Genesis 32:26–28, RSV). The name *Israel* means "He who strives with God," or, as my *Strong's Concordance* has it, "He will rule as God." As dishonest and stumbling as this man Jacob was, God loved him and wanted him to have a fresh start. In no way did he merit election and covenant. It was only because of God's grace that he was given a fresh start.

Somehow all of that is very comforting to me. I fail so often. I'm sometimes dishonest. I stumble a lot in my Christian walk. Yet, like Jacob, I am chosen by God, as are you (John 15:16). We have had a new birth, have become new creatures (2 Corinthians 5:17). Could it be that God has a new name for us, too? Naming is an act of love. We name our children, and then often we give them pet names. Teenagers nickname their closest friends. Lovers often call each other by special names, the meaning of which is sometimes known only to the two of them. Let us at least be open to the possibility of the special grace of being renamed by God at this time of our fresh start! Perhaps you will want to pray for it.

Our Lord said, "To him that overcometh will I give . . . a white stone, and in the stone a new name written, which no man knoweth saving he that receiveth it" (Revelation 2:17). What does that mean? Nineteenth-century writer George MacDonald asserts: "The true name is one which expresses the character, the nature, the being, the *meaning* of the person who bears it."[4] It is the person's own symbol, the picture of one's soul, the sign that belongs to that individual and to no one else. Only God can give it because only He knows the true self within each of us. MacDonald believes that God knows our new name from the beginning but that He reveals it to us only when we can understand and begin to live up to what it signifies.

Who receives a new name? The one who overcomes, who

is victorious. Does that mean that, in order to have a fresh start, we must be perfect? Of course not. But we must at the very least be working toward being who God created us to be. We must offer God our selfhood, claim our birthright by seeing that we are *"one* of God's children, *this* one of the Father's making." As MacDonald points out, no one else can worship God as you do, and no one else can understand Him in quite the same way that you do. The new name is a symbol of that uniqueness, and of the *individuality* of your relationship with God.

Perhaps you'll want to pray that God will reveal your special name to you. I don't know in what way it might become known to you. After I had prayed for that grace, a name seemed to rise up off the page one evening during my Bible reading. I felt immediately that it was mine, but I knew that, as always, if God wanted to tell me something, He would confirm it in more than one way. A few evenings later, during the silent listening part of my prayer time, I seemed to hear the same name called, as if from behind and a little to the right of me.

After this had happened several times in a period of two or three weeks, I felt sure that God had given me a new name. Now, I realize that I could have imagined that, or that it could have happened through the power of suggestion, but that doesn't really matter. Taking that new name as my own and considering it a gift from God seemed to give me a fresh-start awareness more than anything else that had happened to me for a long time. I have held it in my heart as a delicious secret between God and me, and it has become wonderfully precious to me.

It wasn't until very recently, after I'd read MacDonald's sermon, that I realized that the new name has been mine since God created me and that it symbolizes who He wants me to become. I want to keep the name a secret between God and me, but I can tell you that I looked up its meaning, which is: "God is my oath." That nearly took my breath away, because all of my life I've had a powerful sense that the great lesson of my life is to learn to be true—true to God, true to others, true to myself. Now I have a solid sense of the *ideal me* that God is still working to create. It's all right that I'm far from that ideal. The name is a reminder and an inspiration, a mold that can form me into the person God created me to be. As MacDonald writes, "Let him [God] call me what he will. The name shall be precious as my life." Amen. Amen.

Developing New Patterns

With our fresh-start attitude, we can develop new patterns for moving into the future. There's a tendency, especially as we grow older, to think that everything must be done exactly as we've always done it. Alarm, get up, bathroom, coffee on, fix breakfast, read paper, and so on. Now, I know there's a comfortableness about routine, and that's all to the good. Who wants to make decisions at 6:45 A.M., anyway? But now and then, I find it invigorating to deliberately change old routines, just for the sake of experiencing my own aliveness. Isn't that why we take vacations, or days off, or go to the beach, or the mountains, or camp out somewhere? I'll admit that I don't always keep a fresh-start consciousness, but here are some things that help me regain it when it's temporarily lost.

One of the best builders of a fresh-start attitude is using biblical affirmations. For instance, as soon as you wake up in the morning, say to yourself, "This is the day the Lord hath made. I will rejoice and be glad in it." There are so many marvelous biblical affirmations, appropriate for every situation of the day. In Appendix Two, you'll find a list of some of these. You may want to write them on cards and place them around the house or office, or tape-record them to listen to as you're falling asleep at night, or as you're driving, or doing any task that doesn't require concentration. Living with God's *active* affirmations can have a profound effect on your daily life. I hope you'll decide to try it!

A fresh-start consciousness can also be cultivated by varying your habitual routines. Whenever I do heavy cleaning, I like to change the furniture arrangements. There's something about that difference that gives me the feel of a new environment. It keeps waking me up to newness, reminding me that I'm making a fresh start, calling up those words of Paul, "If any one is in Christ, he is a new creation; the old has passed away, behold, the new has come" (2 Corinthians 5:17, RSV).

Going a different route to work can do the same thing. Try turning a couple of streets ahead of where you habitually turn. Alert your senses to pay attention to the sights and sounds and scents you rarely see because you usually go the other way. Remind yourself whose creation this is. Or, maybe sometimes you can get up a little earlier and walk to work or to the bus or subway or store or park. I've found that walking gives me a completely different perspective on the streets I normally drive down every day.

When I ask retreat participants to take prayer walks, many of them come back with glowing faces, reporting that it somehow awakened the child in them. I think this happens because we adults have become so used to driving everywhere we go that we've forgotten what God's world looks like up close!

Asking "Why Not?"

Whenever we hear ourselves saying, "I could never do that," or, "Maybe someday I'll try it, but not now," or, "I've never done it that way before," we need to talk back to ourselves and say, *"Why not?"* Sometimes there's a good reason, of course, but often there isn't.

We've been going to our mountain cabin as a family every summer for as long as I can remember. But four years ago I had a work project for which I needed an island of time and space. I thought about going to the cabin alone, but that can't-do-it voice in my head said, "Eight hours is too long for me to drive all alone. Besides, it would be scary at the cabin with no one else there. And how would my family get along while I was gone? Oh, I couldn't possibly go." But God, who made me a new creature, also empowers me to face uncertainties, and I sensed He wanted me to do this. So I talked back to that voice in my head and said, right out loud in my empty kitchen, *"Well, why not?"*

So I drove to Colorado, most of the way in pouring rain, but just as I headed west out of Limon and the paving turned red from that wonderful Colorado rocky soil, the sun broke through, and the most marvelous rush of LOVE came over me. The flatlands, the cows grazing, sun streaming in rays through the cumulus clouds, the distant mountains painted purple against the sky—oh, what peace they brought to my soul. I laughed out loud, sang, chanted, thanked God. I remember thinking, *If I had only this one moment out of a lifetime, it would have been worth being born for.* At the cabin that night, I wrote in my journal:

> Long trips are usually tension-builders for me, but this was an *unwinding* time. I felt such a lifting of the heaviness of the past year. It was as if I were going to some kind of secret rendezvous—only the one I was meeting was God. In many ways, I have been away from Him—and from my deepest self—for so very long. This is a glorious *homecoming.* I have a marvelous inner awareness of *connecting* with my lost self, of becoming one and true and whole. Something strong in me is saying, "Go for God and don't worry about all the rest."
>
> O Lord, I ask You to come to me in all Your marvelous invisibility and mystery, to heal and make me whole. What I'm really asking is that You keep reminding me to *go for You,* knowing I can depend on You to get me safely through whatever narrow passages I have to face.

As I settled into the cabin, I discovered that I was not alone at all. The One who said, "Lo, I am with you always" was more truly real to me during that week than He'd ever been before. My stay alone at the cabin was so very precious to me that I've made it an annual time-apart that truly feeds my hungering soul. As I write this, I'm sitting at the dining table, looking at the pine-covered mountains, soaking up what they teach me anew every year about God—that there is strength, protection, holiness, in this place . . . and in Him.

If there's something you'd like to do but your can't-do-it voice says "No," *talk back,* remembering that you've got an invisible partner who has made you a new creation. Choose to risk. Within that adventure, there may be a moment so precious that it is worth being born for.

Starting Fresh at Any Age

In my heart I still think of myself as about twenty-five, but there are certain little signs that are getting harder and harder to ignore, such as the age spots (horrors!) appearing on my hands, the slower pace with which I climb the mountain behind our cabin, and my little granddaughter's recent remark, "Grandma, your face is getting crinkly!"

Yesterday, after a nine-hour drive by myself, I ordered a hamburger at a fast-food place, and the cashier said, "Senior Citizen?" Now folks, that term means sixty-five, and I'm only(!) fifty-seven. If that incident had happened a year or so ago, I probably would have felt insulted or hurt, but yesterday I just laughed and said, "Well, I guess this has been a longer day than I thought!" I continued to chuckle over the young woman's question all evening. I think the change in my attitude about aging has come because I've been thinking a lot lately about Mrs. Moore.

"Ganga" (our daughter's name for this lovely neighbor lady) must have been in her late seventies when she started baby-sitting with eighteen-month-old Karen two mornings a week so I could teach a couple of college classes. Even with all the mature wisdom of her years, Mrs. Moore had never lost her own childlike nature. She and Karen played together, laughed together, and learned new things together every day.

One day when I came home, Karen had broken a thermometer and those two girls (the grown-up one and the baby) were sitting at the kitchen table giggling and playing with the mercury, watching it jump back into a state of complete oneness, even though it had been scattered in tiny droplets all over the table. Then Mrs. Moore said, "This is the most fun I've had in years. Too bad people aren't more like mercury. We could be, you know!"

Mrs. Moore had a fresh-start attitude. She was always looking for new things to learn, stubbornly refusing to let her chronological age interfere with her ability to grow. One day, "Ganga" told me she'd been asked to give a program about birds for an organization she belonged to. "Well," she said to me, "I don't know one thing about birds—so *of course* I said I would!"

For the next few weeks, she was in a state of wonder every time she came to our house. "Did you know that birds have an air sac that helps them to fly? That's part of their secret! Imagine! Isn't that exciting?" She showed Karen and me pictures of all kinds of birds, and diagrams of their bodies with explanations of how they fly. Then one day she said, "You know, it's that empty space within that makes it possible for a bird to fly. Maybe, if each of us kept an empty space within, a silent, holy room where Christ could lay His head, *our spirits* could fly!"

Clearly, this was a lady with a fresh-start attitude, who truly *lived* until the day she died. I've been told that, on the gray February day on which she was buried, a box of seed packets she'd ordered arrived in the mail. I have no doubt that Mrs. Moore's entrance into heaven was strewn with hyacinths and daisies, and that her eyes sparkled with anticipation at all she was about to discover.

You and I can have a fresh-start attitude, too, and one of the things that will contribute to that is to consciously choose to let go of our fears about aging. Like Mrs. Moore, we can keep reminding ourselves that there are *always* things to look forward to, always more wonders to learn about, always new ways to grow. What new thing could you try today? It doesn't have to be anything big (although it *could* be). But maybe you'd just like to look up something in the encyclopedia, or try a new game, or go for a walk in a place you've never walked before.

For those who have a fresh-start attitude, there is a certain wisdom and grace in maturity that is every bit as appealing as young beauty. I think I'm going to give up trying to stall my advancing years. I truly wouldn't want to be twenty—or thirty—or forty—or even fifty again. *This* is the right age for living, crinkly face and all! I hope that, like Mrs. Moore, I can keep that attitude all my life. Maybe I can, if I keep reminding myself that the One who beckons me to keep growing is the One who also *moves on with me.*

Learning to Fly

When I was in my early forties, my husband's architectural firm offered to pay for flying lessons for me so that I could fly Rex around on his many out-of-town trips. First I went to ground school to learn the basics, and then I started flying with an instructor. After I'd logged many hours in the air with my teacher, one crisp fall day I made an almost-perfect landing. As we taxied down the runway, Mr. Shaner said, "Would you come to a complete stop, please?" I was surprised, because we'd been doing touch-and-go take-offs and landings, but I did as he asked. As soon as the airplane came to a stop, my instructor opened his door, shook my hand, and said, "She's all yours. Paint her on!" (That's pilot talk for a smooth landing.) Then he got out of the airplane.

He was asking me to solo! My first reaction was absolute terror. *Oh no, I can't do it. I'm not ready for this!* I looked out the window, shaking my head at him, but my instructor just stood there smiling and waving, with a look of absolute confidence on his face.

Well, okay, I thought, *here goes nothing!* I took a deep breath, revved up the engine, and gunned it down the runway, then gently pulled back on the wheel. I'll never forget the moment of lift-off, the slow, rising flight into the sky, and the exhilaration I felt when I realized I was airborne. "I can fly! I can fly!" I shouted in the empty cabin.

Then it hit me. I was going to have to land this thing by myself. I had no choice now. There was absolutely no way to get out of it. With my heart pounding wildly, I made the necessary turns, lined up with the runway, cut the throttle, and glided gently toward the ground, pulling back just before touching down. I'd like to say it was another perfect landing but it wasn't. I bounced on impact, but that didn't matter at all now. I had done it! I could fly! When I taxied back to where my instructor was waiting, I was in a state of absolute euphoria. I felt like a new being. I could fly, I could fly, I could fly!

What if I'd listened to my own fears instead of trusting my teacher's confidence in me? I might never have built up the courage to solo. When something unexpected is thrust upon us, very often our first emotion is fear. We think of what we have to lose. But there are two sides to every experience of change. You let go of something, but you also gain something you didn't have before. There is a gift in every change, if we look for it. I think that the *unexpected* changes especially are ways in which God grows us toward what He wants us to be. If you and I could begin to see every experience of change as both a loss and a gain and embrace them both, we'd find new hope for our living.

So let's affirm together, at this moment, that every exit is also an entrance, that our sins are forgiven, that we do indeed have a fresh, new start. As we unwrap all the gifts of God's grace and learn to claim and accept them, let's keep remembering to reinstate, renew, reaffirm our fresh-start attitude, so that finally, because of Christ, we can come to the end of each day shouting in our hearts, *I can fly, I can fly, I can fly!*

NOTES

1. William Blake, "Eternity."

2. John Claypool, from a taped talk given at a Montreat Conference on Worship and Music, Montreat, North Carolina, June 1985.

3. In a video presentation entitled *The Taste of New Wine,* Keith Miller uses this image to show that, like a beach ball we're trying to hold under water, our unprocessed pain keeps bobbing up again. Not only is this process hopeless, but it also wastes a tremendous amount of energy that could be going into our fresh start.

4. George MacDonald, "The New Name," *Unspoken Sermons:* Series One (London: Alexander Strahan, 1867), pp. 100–117.

CHAPTER 3

The Gift
of Being Real

The truth shall make you free.

John 8:32

Jessica was four years old, and she loved her tall, spindly-legged Grandpa (whom she called Pompo) very much. Pompo, who lived with Jessica and her parents, had curly black hair with a streak of gray that tumbled onto his forehead when he got down on all fours and let himself be Jessica's horse. The two of them spent many carefree hours together. Sometimes in the summer Pompo took Jessica fishing with him by the river. She loved to watch his bobbers for him, and squealed with delight when he let her reel in a flopping fish. In the fall, Pompo and Jessica walked around the neighborhood collecting pretty leaves, and Pompo taught Jessica the names of all the trees and how to recognize them by their leaves. On winter nights, he often held her on his lap by the fire and read to her from a book by Hans Christian Andersen that Pompo said had been his when he was a boy. When Shirley, her favorite doll, lost an arm, Jessica went crying to Pompo and he made Shirley well again.

But one fall day, just as the maple leaves were turning red and starting to fall, Jessica's mother took Pompo to the doctor. After that, something strange happened in Jessica's house. Her parents started to whisper, and often when Pompo came into the room, they'd stop talking altogether. There seemed to be a big secret hanging in the air like a heavy water balloon about to burst. Always before, the family had talked together about whatever came up, but now Pompo and Jessica seemed to be left out. It felt *awful!*

Pompo got thinner and thinner, and his face turned gray, and then he started staying in bed all day instead of playing with Jessica. When she asked her parents about it, they said, "It's okay, dear. Pompo is just getting old and he's kind of sick, like when you had the flu last winter. But he'll be all right one of these days." They kept saying the same kinds of things to Pompo.

Then one night Jessica lay tossing and turning on her bed. She could hear her parents talking quietly in the kitchen, so she got up and tiptoed out of her room. Just before she got to the kitchen door, she heard her father say, "Look, Marian. Your dad is dying. You've just got to face that fact. He has only a couple of weeks left, at best."

Very quietly, Jessica tiptoed back to her room. Even though she was only four years old, she'd somehow known that all along. Why had they shut her and Pompo out? It was awful to know that Pompo was dying, but it was even worse not to be able to talk to anyone about it. Jessica lay there a long time, and then she knew what she had to do. She sneaked out of bed and went into Pompo's room and woke him up. "Please don't die, Pompo!" she cried.

Pompo blinked his eyes and then reached out a frail arm and put it around Jessica. "Look, Baby. I don't want to die. I don't want to go away from you, but I know that I *am* dying. Your mommy and daddy think I don't know it, but I do. I'm going to be with God, but I'll always love you. Always." Jessica put Pompo's rough hand over her face and cried into it.

After a while, Jessica stopped crying and looked up. Her parents were standing in the doorway. Suddenly, Jessica realized that she and Pompo had broken the spell of the secret, and she was afraid of being punished. For a moment her mother stood there, looking stiff and stern. Then she seemed to melt. She knelt down by Jessica and hugged her and Pompo. "Thank God," she said. "Thank God the truth is out."

Then they all began to talk about dying and what it would be like for Pompo in heaven, and how hard it would be for all of them when he died. It hurt, but it also felt good to be able to talk about it. The secret didn't seem quite so terrible now that they were all in it together.

Pompo died a couple of weeks later. Jessica is a woman now, but she still remembers the good feeling of that night when she and her family broke through the secret and started being honest with each other. And even now, whenever Jessica goes fishing with her husband, or reads by the fire, or gathers leaves in the fall, she thinks of a curly-haired, spindly-legged man called Pompo, whose death taught her the value of "getting the truth out."[1]

The Key to True Spiritual Growth

Honesty. It's so natural for children and old people, but most of us learn somewhere between childhood and our teen years to hide quite a bit of our own truth. It's partly because we feel such a strong need for the approval of others. I know that I often wear masks of one kind or another. Lately, though, I've been working on getting rid of some of them, because I have come to believe that *this is one of the most important things I can do for the health of my body, soul, and spirit.* It's also the highway map that charts the course to better relationships with other people and with God.

Jesus said that "unless you turn and become like children, you will never enter the kingdom of heaven" (Matthew 18:3, RSV). The most noticeable characteristic of small children is that they are completely honest. They say what they think, express their feelings without hesitation, smile when they're happy, and frown or cry when they're angry or sad. They do not try to hide who they are. There's a wonderful word for this characteristic—*congruency.* It means that our words and actions match our inner truth. I'm quite sure that's what Jesus was asking us to strive for.

But isn't it an impossible goal? Yes. It is impossible, just as it is not possible for a camel to pass through the eye of a needle. Yet Jesus reminds us, as He did His disciples, that "things which are impossible with men are possible with God" (Luke 18:24; see also Matthew 19:23–26; Mark 10:23–27). Therein lies the *grace* of it. I know that it's impossible for me to be congruent by my own efforts. I learned that by trying and trying and failing and failing. That's why the gift of being real truly is a grace—perhaps the one of greatest value, because only through childlike honesty are we made able to enter the kingdom of God!

Children do get rather quickly trained out of their heart-level honesty, and to some extent that's necessary. When our son John was about two years old, he said to a lady who was helping me with some cleaning, "Mrs. H., you've got *B.O.!*" Mrs. H. did *not* appreciate that remark a whole lot! There are certain amenities that are necessary. You would not walk down the street with your clothes off or poke a friend in a wounded place. Neither would you bare your soul to everyone you meet, nor deliberately hurt another person in the name of honesty. So it is necessary to wear a mask now and then; but the essential thing is to be aware of those masks and to realize that they are not who we are.

Recently, the idea of congruency between the inner and the outer person has been coming to me from many directions. When apparent coincidences happen in my life, I've learned to pay attention because it usually signals something that God wants me to be working on for my own spiritual growth.

The Healing Power in Honest Emotions

I started becoming aware of my own unrealness about a year ago, when my daughter was having difficulty with depression. (Karen has given me permission to tell some of her story in the hope that it may help others.) One of the things I kept reading concerning depression is that it's often anger turned inward. When people are afraid to express their honest feelings, whatever those might be, they tend to turn the feelings in upon themselves. For most of my life, I've had a strong tendency to hold in my negative feelings, which then came out in the form of migraine headaches. Because Karen didn't see me expressing much anger, she got the unspoken message that anger was not an acceptable emotion. She was our easiest child to raise—always cooperative and pleasant, wearing a smile, doing nice things for others, excelling in school. She had a part-time job during high school, and the people she worked with nicknamed her Sunshine. But oh, the cost was much too high. When she became a young adult, she fell into depression, for no *apparent* reason. In therapy, she learned that during all of those years of outward pleasantness, she had been swallowing her own negative emotions. Finally, the accumulation became too great, and she suffered from depression.

Karen is now working on getting her negative emotions out. She's learning that there are ways to do this without hurting others. (In chapter 9, we'll talk about some of these ways, because we all sometimes swallow emotions.) The point here is that being honest about your feelings is one of the healthiest things you can do for your body, soul, and spirit.

As a part of her therapy, I was asked to come in for some sessions with Karen and her therapist, Mona. The first thing Mona said when the three of us were together was, "There's only one thing I ask of family members, and that's honesty." As the sessions progressed, I found myself sometimes avoiding saying exactly how I felt about something because I was afraid of hurting Karen's feelings. Mona, being a very sensitive therapist, picked up on these evasions and kept asking me questions such as, "Is that *really* how you feel about it? Please be honest, now." Sometimes even then I found it hard to get the words out.

Then Mona made a statement that I had trouble believing at first but I've now come by experience to know is true. This is what she said: "I have never seen the verbal expression of honest emotions destroy a relationship. Never. No matter what the emotions are. What destroys relationships is dishonesty. Hard truths are always easier to take than the uncertainty and insecurity of being unsure whether or not the other person means what she's saying."

One day, when I got home after a particularly difficult session, I went into the bedroom, closed the door, and wrote at the top of a page in a notebook: "Well, at least I can be honest with myself. Here's how I really feel." Then I wrote down all the emotions I was feeling but was afraid to express to Karen for fear of hurting her. I arrived early for our next session and when I showed Mona my notebook page she said, "Karen really needs to hear these things from you. If you can't say them, maybe you could read to her from what you've written."

So when Karen arrived, I took a deep breath and then read what I'd written. It would be nice to be able to say that my daughter understood my feelings and accepted them right away, but it didn't happen that way. She was upset and angry and, most of all, hurt, and we left the session that way. By the next week, though, we were able to talk about the emotions I'd expressed and about Karen's feelings that came in response to mine. With Mona's help, we just kept processing our feelings, and by the end of the session, Karen and I were hugging each other, with tears of relief running down our faces. It felt like a homecoming. In many ways, it was.

Since then, I've been trying very hard to be more honest about my feelings. For example, Karen recently asked me to drive to a nearby town with her to shop. I was tired and didn't really want to go, but I said okay because I didn't want to disappoint her. As I started toward the bedroom to change clothes, she said, "Mom. Do you really want to go or are you just doing it to please me?"

I thought about it a moment and then said, "I guess I really want to stay home and take a nap." We both laughed, and then Karen said, "See? It works! I'd lots rather have it this way than to have you go and resent it."

A Word of Caution: There are three things to keep in mind when you're trying to be honest about feelings. First, don't dredge up past garbage. Express only what you're feeling *now.* Second, do not verbally attack or criticize or analyze the other person. Say only what *your* feelings are. Third, be sure that what you're expressing really is an emotion. (To say, "I feel you are too impatient" is *not* expressing a feeling, even though the word *feel* is in the sentence.) If your relationship is in serious trouble, or if you have deep-seated emotional scars, you'll probably need professional help with this. Just remember, if you do have counseling, to keep God involved in the process. I am convinced that there is no true healing without Him.

The Illuminating Power of Honest Words

About the same time that Karen and I were working on our problems, a new friend came into my life. Jan is a person who places honesty very near the top of her list of values. I liked her immediately. When people *are* just who they *are,* you can sense it. Their basic honesty shines through and draws people to them. Seeing her made me want to be that way, too, so I asked God to help me become more honest. Guess how He's doing it? By making me aware of the many ways in which I'm *dis*honest!

Oh, I don't mean that I go around deliberately telling lies or stealing or cheating on my income tax. It's just that, in my strong need for the approval of others, I sometimes say things I don't really mean. For example, I've been catching myself more often when I say flattering things—something I didn't used to give a second thought to. The Bible says, "A flattering mouth works ruin" (Proverbs 26:28, RSV). That's a pretty strong statement, isn't it? I mean, gee whiz, what does it hurt to tell someone you like her new hair style, even if you don't? Where's the "ruin" in that? The reason why flattery is ruinous is that, on some deep level, the person knows you don't really mean it. Then it becomes hard to trust anything you say. This distrust leads to confusion, which is a state of mind that belongs to the darkness, not the light. In fact, here's something very exciting that I've begun to sense: *when your words are deeply honest, they scatter spiritual light around you.* When they are insincere or dishonest, a darkness envelops you that other people sense, although they might not be able to name it.

Of course, we can be taken in by flattery, but only when we consciously or unconsciously *choose* to be. This, then, leads to false pride. So flattery, which seems to be such a harmless little bug, turns out to be a coiled snake.

And yet the Bible also suggests that we should "build each other up." (See Acts 20:32.) What is the difference between building up and flattery? I used to try to build my children up by praising every paper they brought home from school.

Then when Karen was in junior high, she wrote an essay for a contest. Please excuse my maternal pride, but it truly was an excellent piece for an eighth grader, and I told her so. But Karen didn't want to enter it in the contest. When I asked her why, she said, "You say it's good, but you say that about everything I do. How do I know whether or not it's worth submitting?" Oooo, ouch! A painful truth!

On the other hand, haven't you known people who compliment so rarely that, when they do say something nice, you *know* they mean it? That's better than blanket flattery, of course, but people who live or work with those who are stingy with their kind words sometimes feel starved for affirmation.

How, then, can we build each other up without being dishonest, without creating confusion? Here's what I've noticed about Jan. She says a lot of nice things to people, but I've observed that she waits until she finds one specific thing that she truly likes and then says only that. For example, she and I recently listened to a speaker whose material was not very interesting. It seemed to me that the talk went on and on and on. Afterwards, I caught myself (a few seconds too late!) shaking the speaker's hand and saying, "Thanks a lot. I really enjoyed that." As I walked away I thought, *Now why did I say that? I didn't really enjoy that talk. That was dishonest of me.* Then I heard Jan say to the speaker, "One phrase of yours really stands out for me." Then she repeated a four-word phrase that truly *was* creative and memorable. That was all she said, but I'm sure Jan's words gave him a warm glow because they were specific and because he knew they were true!

I have done quite a bit of public speaking, and I've found that you know, somehow, whether or not the audience is responsive to what you've said. When I've felt a talk falling flat, it makes me feel even worse to have people come up and shake my hand and say "I really enjoyed that." But when someone picks out a specific thing that they found meaningful, it seems to give me wings! This is true not only in regard to speeches and performances but also in day-to-day interactions with other people. I'm learning from Jan that, if we are attentive to other people, we can *always* find something to say that is true and therefore validating. We can build each other up by *truth* and surround ourselves and them in light at the same time.

The Freeing Power of Being True

Another failing that God has been calling to my attention since I asked Him to help me to become more real is this: I sometimes find myself agreeing with someone and only later realizing that, in fact, my position on the issue was quite different from theirs. If you're a people-pleaser, you may understand that this kind of dishonesty comes from my extreme need for approval and my fear of conflict. But that does not make it acceptable. In fact, pretending to agree actually *decreases* self-esteem.

This was brought to my attention a while back in a way that shocked me. I was talking with two friends who have very differing views about a particular issue within our church. After one of them had expressed her viewpoint, she turned to me and said, "I know that Marilyn agrees with me." The other friend looked shocked and said, "I thought she agreed with *me!*" We laughed, I made some noncommittal comment, and the conversation continued. But something in me winced at the stab of my own incongruity. Suddenly, I felt like a great big fake!

When I got home, I went to my quiet place and talked to God about it. Then I asked myself where I honestly stood on the issue. My position was somewhere *between* that of my two friends. But how could I admit to them my failure to be faithful to my inner truth? What if they got mad at me? I know that sounds childish, but my childhood experiences created in me a fear of anger that is not always logical. Then I remembered Paul's words in 1 Thessalonians 2:4 (JB), "When we are speaking, we are not trying to please men but God, who can read our inmost thoughts." *Oh yes,* I thought. *When I try to please everybody, I end up pleasing nobody!*

After praying for moral strength, I called up both friends and apologized, explaining my *true* position. One of them was very accepting, but the other expressed some anger about discovering that I didn't fully agree with her after all. But do you know what I discovered? I could stand her anger better than I could stand my own deception! I am coming to believe that the very worst kind of enemy is the enemy within, that part of me that betrays my own deepest truth. That morning after I made the phone calls, I knew the absolutely solid validity of Christ's words, "ye shall know the truth, and the truth shall make you free" (John 8:32). There is no freedom without truth. Suddenly it seemed that the child in me, that part who *is* who she is, started to dance and shout and clap her hands. In that moment I knew that the treasure was worth all of the struggle, for the only way I'd ever enter the kingdom of God was by diligently working, all of my life, to become that child who dances in the light of truth.

The Cleansing Power of Facing Our Darkness

So it's true that every one of us wears masks of one kind or another. We all hide behind false fronts. But once we've asked God to help us get rid of them, we need to pray for the courage to follow through. Sometimes that's the hardest part, but it's the one thing that will bring us the greatest measure of grace if we can stay with it. So let's turn now to some of those tough situations that need to be faced if we are to claim the gift of being real.

Clearing Away the Smog

Just as a lingering smog that hovers over a large city can be a far greater hazard than a violent thunderstorm, it's the little half-truths, the almost-right words, the slight distortions of facts, that are ultimately the most damaging to individuals and to relationships. The out-and-out blatant dishonesties are terrible, but at least they are easily seen for what they are.

Here's an example of gray smog, an incident told to me by a friend. One evening when she was having dinner with some friends at their house, the wife asked her husband, "Did Bill call you today?" The husband answered immediately, "No. He sure didn't." Later in the evening, the phone rang and the wife answered it. It was Bill, and he said, "Earlier today when I was talking to your husband. . . ." After she hung up, the wife said to her husband, "I asked you if Bill had called and you said no. Why did you lie to me?" The husband's reply was, "I wasn't lying. Bill didn't call me. I called him."

Even though he had answered her question correctly, the husband misled his wife. He really was being dishonest because he intended to deceive her. Maybe he didn't want to discuss the matter in front of my friend, and that's okay. But for his own integrity, as well as that of his wife and friend, he needed to say that. It would have been a simple matter to say, "He didn't call me, so I called him. We can talk about it later this evening."

I don't know what the situation was, but maybe it was something the husband simply didn't want to tell his wife about. In that case, he still could have been honest by saying, "I talked to Bill, but I just don't want to discuss the conversation." That's hard. It's really hard. But preserving one's integrity is worth the struggle.

Another form of gray smog is making excuses for saying no, instead of giving the true reason for your refusal. Once when my children were small, I had accepted an invitation to a bridge party, but as the day drew near, I began to feel bad about leaving the children. Some unexpected things had caused me to be away from home several times that week. I dreaded calling the hostess on such short notice and leaving her in the lurch, but I knew my children needed me to be at home. So, fearing that the hostess would be angry with me and not understand my reason, I called and told her the babysitter had backed out. Ten minutes later, she called back and said, "I've got it all worked out. I found another sitter for you!" So I ended up going to the party and, worst of all, leaving my children with a woman they'd never seen before. Well, I'm sure you see where my many mistakes were. I still need to remind myself of that incident whenever I'm tempted to give a made-up excuse for saying no, instead of telling the true reason.

Maybe it won't make a lot of difference to the other person, but one thing is sure. It will make a difference within you. *Honesty in little things builds inner truth.* Just this morning, a friend told me that a woman had called and asked her to give a TV interview to promote a musical series that my friend felt was not going to be a good line-up. She told the woman no and was honest about her reason. When I said,

"That must have been hard to say," she said, "Yes. It was, but I knew I had to be true to myself." That kind of honesty builds self-esteem. I could sense that in my friend; and I hope that I can learn to live closer to my own truth, too. This friend has truly claimed the priceless gift of being real, and her example is a *grace* in my life, urging me to try to be more true. I know it's worth my most earnest effort.

Gray smog, unrecognized, can cause a person's self-respect to sicken and die. But the good news is that Jesus Christ came "not to call the righteous, but sinners to repentance" (Luke 5:31–32). If you can see your own part in creating gray smog, admit it, and work toward living your own truth, the air will come clean again—as fresh and clear as a rainbow day in May.

Getting Rid of the Junk

Somewhere I read the statement that spiritual growth is *simply becoming more aware.* Perhaps that's true. When I'm able to look at my hidden motivations and little dishonesties without wallowing in guilt or condemning myself, an amazing thing happens. I discover that God does not condemn me, either. We can all identify with the freedom and relief the adulterous woman surely felt when Jesus said, "Neither do I condemn thee: go, and sin no more" (John 8:11).

On the other hand, if I'm afraid to look at the darkness in my own mental basement, I have absolutely no chance of growing spiritually. What really holds us back from being more aware is the fear of what we will see if we truly look at ourselves. Yet what are we afraid of? God already knows what's there. And here's the crux of it: when we are aware of our dark side (and we do all have a dark side), we then have the option of expressing either darkness or light. We truly have a choice. *But* . . . if we do not recognize the negative junk in our basements, *it will come out anyway!* It will come creeping up the back stairs in subtle ways; and then one day we'll look around and say, "How come my life is such a mess?"

One quality we often stuff into our mental basements is anger. And one of the commonest ways repressed anger comes out is in passive-aggressive behavior. For example, the child who "drives her mother crazy" by dawdling over her food, the husband who "forgets" to mail his wife's letter to her mother, or the wife who embarrasses her punctual husband by making them late to social gatherings *may* be expressing anger that they've been stuffing down inside themselves. Unexpressed anger may come out in sarcastic remarks that just absolutely flatten another person, or in talking about people behind their backs, or in actions that have nasty edges to them.

Years ago, when I lived in an apartment with two other first-year teachers, one roommate was dating a young widower who had not fully recovered from the death of his first wife. Mike sent Joyce a dozen roses on Valentine's Day— eleven red ones and one white one. The white rose was for his wife. Joyce was hurt by this. I won't debate whether or not her feelings were appropriate. Feelings just are. But instead of telling Bill how that made her feel, she put the white rose in the oven for a couple of minutes and then stuck it back in the bouquet, wilted and drooping. That's passive-aggressive. When Mike came over that evening, the couple didn't talk about the rose or Joyce's feelings, but the tension in the air was suffocating. Mike thanked us for dinner, then asked for his coat and left, never to return. Joyce made her point, but she lost Mike.

Passive-aggressive words and acts wouldn't be necessary if we could learn to deal with our anger as it comes up. The important thing in doing this is to take responsibility for our own feelings, rather than blame the other person. For example, to say "I'm feeling really angry right now and I need to talk about my feelings," is not pointing a finger at the other person. However, to say "You make me so mad I could scream," makes the other person defensive. Once angry feelings are worked through, they can be let go of. Then they won't come out in passive-aggressive ways.

Cleaning the Windows of Our Self-Image

Another thing that happens when we refuse to look at our inner darkness is that we may overcompensate for it. For example, if you have a secret fear that you may be a selfish person, you might try to hide that from yourself and others by continually giving up your own needs and wants in favor of those of others. You may become either a martyr or a doormat or both. Yet, if you're able to admit to yourself that there is some selfishness in you, along with your more altruistic qualities, you can take care of your own needs, *which actually frees you for the important business of helping others.* Certainly Jesus intended for us to do this. When people crowded in on Him too closely, He did not hesitate to say, in effect, "Enough! I need to get away by myself for a while!" (See Matthew 14:13 and 23.) He knew that He could serve other people effectively *only* if He took some time for Himself.

It is very important to become aware of one's own dark side and own it. That is the one insight that has helped me more than anything else in my ongoing struggle for realness. During Karen's hospitalization, we attended weekly group sessions in which family members and patients talked about their feelings and their problems. I found myself getting upset whenever a therapist or family member or other person in the group made the slightest suggestion that my actions and words were not *always* one hundred percent loving and caring. One evening, when I started crying about a remark of this kind, the therapist said, "You wouldn't be reacting so strongly if you weren't afraid that it might be true."

Oh! I felt as if I'd been stabbed in the heart! I was hurt and angry and I just wanted *out* of that room! I cried off and on for several days. Some time during the following week, the psalm assigned in the daily Bible reading program I follow was Psalm 139. These words seemed to drop way down into some deep place in me: "Search me, O God, and know my heart! Try me and know my thoughts! And see if there be any wicked way in me, and lead me in the way everlasting!" I prayed those words over and over, as my prayer. Then I went to bed and found myself lying awake, unable to sleep.

Suddenly, something within me said, "Yes! There *is* an unloving, uncaring part of me. Yes. There *is.* God, You already know it. Now I'm admitting it to You."

I can't find the words to tell you the kind of relief I felt, once I had admitted to God my secret fear. I had struggled and struggled against that awareness most of my life, over-compensating by trying to be everything to everybody.

Now, here's the wonder of it. Once I faced my darkness and accepted it as part of me, I discovered that it was just that—only a *very small part* of me. Then I could see that there was also a deeply loving, caring part of me . . . and that it far overreached the unloving part. By the grace of God, the light was greater than the darkness. What followed was pure gift. Once I recognized this aspect of my shadow side, my fear of it started to abate. I think it's slowly losing its power to force me into being unreal.

I've come to see that everybody has some unloving, uncaring feelings and thoughts and that, as long as you can't admit them to yourself, you'll either act them out in passive-aggressive ways or else overcompensate, as I did. But once you see your dark side, you truly have a choice about how you're going to act. Human relations consultants Muriel James and Dorothy Jongeward wrote,

> Authentic persons do not dedicate their lives to a concept of what they imagine they *should* be; rather, they are themselves and as such do not use their energy putting on a performance, maintaining pretense, manipulating others.[2]

Of course, that doesn't mean that you do whatever feels good. Aware of your own darkness, you choose the light; and the light overcomes the darkness. Living a congruent life, you truly become what and who God created you to be. And that's the pulsing, breathing grace of a life that's real.

NOTES

1. This is a fictional story based on truth. Names and some details have been changed to protect the persons involved.

2. Muriel James and Dorothy Jongeward, *Born to Win* (New York: The New American Library, 1971), p. 2.

CHAPTER 4

The Gift of Intimacy with God

If anyone hears my voice and opens the door, I will come in and eat with him, and he with me.

Revelation 3:20, NIV

During part of World War II, my father was stationed at the Naval Air Technical Training Center in Chicago. I was in the eighth grade when Mother and I moved from our home on a friendly, tree-lined street in McCook, Nebraska, to an apartment in the Windy City and I started school there.

It was quite an adjustment to go from a small town where everyone knew everything about everyone else, to a city where people passed each other every day without speaking. Each morning, I'd walk a few blocks and stand on a street corner that was sandwiched between tall brick apartment buildings, to catch the school bus. I usually arrived about five minutes early and stood at the edge of a group of laughing, talking, young people who simply ignored me. After the first couple of days, though, I realized that there was another girl and a boy who, like me, stared at their shoes while they waited. We never looked directly at each other, never spoke, never smiled.

One day in late November the bus was late, and it started to sprinkle. Then a gust of wind made me wrap my coat tighter. Without looking up, we three outsiders moved a step or two closer to each other for warmth. I noticed that the girl had on a pair of saddle shoes that were exactly the kind I'd been looking for. I wondered where she'd bought them. *Why not ask her?* I thought. But I couldn't. The boy pulled a yo-yo out of his pocket and began playing with it. He was good! *Why not tell him I'd been practicing with a yo-yo, too?* I couldn't.

Then, suddenly, a little cocker spaniel puppy escaped from the apartment building behind us and came running right over to the three of us, wagging his tail. The boy picked him up and started petting him. "He looks like *my* dog!" I blurted out, before I had time to think about whether or not I could dare to say it.

"Really?" said the girl, her smile revealing a mouthful of gleaming braces. "I love dogs, too! My dad says that next year we're going to find a house with a yard and real grass, and then we can have a whole back yard full of wet noses and wagging tails!"

"What grade are you in?" the boy asked us, rubbing the puppy's ears as the girl and I petted him. Then questions started tumbling out of all three of us. "What's your name?" "Where do you live?" "What's your favorite subject?" "Do you have brothers and sisters?" "Have you ever been horseback riding?" "Where do you go to church?"

Then there was silence again. Only now it was different. We three were no longer strangers, outsiders. A connection had been made. It was a *grace* moment, and the beginning of a bus-stop friendship that lasted all year. A lady came out to get the puppy just as the bus came. As we stepped onto the bus, I silently thanked God for late buses and rainy winds and little dogs. I was not alone any more.

I think intimacy with God is very much like that break-through moment at the bus stop. It happens when we let our barriers down, when we're not afraid to speak, when we reveal something of ourselves to God and allow Him to reveal Himself to us. It assures us that we are no longer alone. It is a grace beyond all others. I know that because, during the times in my life when I'm experiencing intimacy with God, there is an unshakable inner anchor that is completely independent of what's going on externally in my life.

On the other hand, when I slip out of intimacy with Him, my life becomes either dull or unmanageable.

As I write these words, I am experiencing a feather-soft sense of peace such as I have not known for a long time. I cannot tell you what a priceless gift this is to me. For about a year, there has been an overload of stress in my life, as a result of illness in the family and a number of unexpected changes that have had to be worked through. During this time, I have tended to get so caught up in external things that my attention has often been diverted from my personal relationship with God. I hadn't been aware that this was happening until I began to notice a withering of my creativity. Then I looked at the other areas of my life and realized that, in neglecting my relationship with God, I had also become alienated from myself. My life (both internally and externally) had fallen into a state of disorder. But thanks be to God, who comes running to meet His prodigal children, I am beginning to sense a return of intimacy between Him and me. It is a closeness that is more precious to me than mountains and rivers.

I should have known it would happen. Again and again, I have been the prodigal daughter. Sometimes I have left my Father's house to chase worldly goals and dreams. At other times, personal problems have been the lure away from Him. And, like the younger son of Luke 15:11–32, when I've turned away from my Father, I've lost all that was truly precious.

And yet . . . the living, breathing miracle of it is that over and over again, as soon as I make even the least turn toward home, my heavenly Father starts planning a celebration! In spite of my lapses and, yes, partly because of them, I have come to know that my Father's arms are always open to me. He loves me so much that He is faithful, even in the face of my unfaithfulness. I'll never be able to understand that kind of love. I can only accept it.

Focusing on God's Love

Intimacy with God. What a precious gift it is. How, then, can we claim it?

The first step is learning to trust that He really does love us. We don't always know it for sure; we can't always feel it. Yet during the doubting times in my own life, I've found that if I simply choose to believe that my heavenly Father loves me and begin to *direct my attention to Him,* gradually, sometimes imperceptibly at first, I start to be aware of His loving presence again, like a misty rainbow, barely perceptible beyond the storm.

Attention. That's the key. Stephen Gaskin, in *This Season's People,* writes:

> What you put your attention on, you get more of. Each one of us is a fountain of energy, a valve through which life energy is metered into the world. . . . If you put your attention on the best, highest, finest, most beautiful thing that you can, *that* will be amplified for you.[1]

Of course, St. Paul said much the same thing, long before Gaskin did: "Whatsoever things are true, whatsoever things are honest, whatsoever things are just, whatsoever things are pure, whatsoever things are lovely, whatsoever things are of good report; if there be any virtue, and if there be any praise, think on these things" (Philippians 4:8). "For as a [person] thinketh in his heart, so is he" (Proverbs 23:7). It is true. *Attention* is the great secret, the key that will open us to receive the grace of intimacy with God. As you and I direct more and more of our attention toward Him, more and more of His love will flow through us, and our relationship with Him will begin to glow with intimacy.

I found this out a couple of years ago, when I had a virus that I just couldn't seem to shake. Even after all the aches and the fever and the coughing were over, I was still weak and sometimes dizzy. Every day I tried to get up and get going, but after showering, dressing, and brushing my teeth, I'd fall back into bed exhausted.

This had gone on for nearly eight weeks when a friend who came to visit me suggested that, whenever I found myself thinking about my illness, I should use that as a signal to begin meditating on one of the attributes of God, such as His love, His compassion, His power, His mercy. Then I should go around the house (mentally, if not physically), thanking Him for every piece of furniture, every item that I enjoy, for the people in my life, for the sunshine and trees and my car and the air I breathe and whatever else came to mind.

I began to act on her suggestion. And I found that each day I thought of more things to be thankful for. Within only a couple of days, I had begun to sense a wonderful, new companionship with God the Father—*Abba,* Daddy. His presence became almost tangible for me. My body felt lighter, and my energy returned.

Perhaps you'll say that the illness had just run its course and that I might have started feeling better even if I hadn't practiced that spiritual discipline. That may be true, but it's not the point. The point is that focusing my attention on the attributes of God and on my many blessings brought me into a closer relationship with my Lord. And that was the wonderful gift that had been hidden in my adversity, waiting to be claimed! The physical healing was secondary.

Because God is Father, Son, and Holy Spirit, it is possible to develop a close relationship with Him as loving Parent, as divine Friend, and as indwelling Spirit. When I think of Him as Father, I see that He is deeply devoted to me, committed to me, caring, providing, and supporting. He is also the One who sets limits for the good of my soul, calls me back when I wander away, and strengthens me for living. Being a parent myself, I know what tremendous devotion all of that takes. I love my daughter and two sons so much that I'd give them all I have if I thought it would truly make them happy. (It wouldn't, of course.) And yet, if my love were ever tested in that way, would I really give up *everything* for them? Would I, could I, give up even them? It's unthinkable to me. Yet that's what God did. "He that spared not his own Son, but delivered him up for us all, how shall he not with him also freely give us all things?" (Romans 8:32). Knowing how very much I love my own children, how could I possibly doubt my heavenly Father's love for me?

As I meditate on the love of God the Father, one of my earliest memories flashes across my mind. It's a snowy winter night and I've wakened, crying, with a bad earache. My father has gotten up out of his own warm bed, picked me up, and is walking the floor with me, my head resting on his shoulder, my tears dampening the soft folds of his flannel robe. Even now, as that memory rests on my heart like a bird, I feel warm and loved and protected. Amazingly, I cannot recall the pain at all. It is completely gone, erased, swallowed up in the love. Yet my father's love for me is like a grain of sand or a particle of dust compared with God's love for you and me. Who can imagine a Father who loves us enough to give a part of His very being, His own precious Son, in order that you and I might live? (See John 3:16.)

I realize that not everyone is blessed with a loving human father. I have known people who have suffered all of their lives from the lack of their father's love. It may be harder for them to trust the love of God the Father. If you have not known your father, or if your relationship with him is full of pain, try to trust enough to believe this: *you have never truly been without a loving Father.* Never. And you *can* have an intimate relationship with Him, even if you have not known full parental love. " 'Can a woman forget her sucking child, that she should have no compassion on the son of her womb?' *Even these may forget,* yet I will not forget you. Behold, I have graven you on the palms of my hands" (Isaiah 49:15–16, RSV, italics mine).

What does it mean—that you and I are engraved on the palms of God's hands? At a meeting recently, a young woman asked for prayers for her neighbors, and I noticed that another lady there picked up her pen and started writing on the palm of her hand. Later, I learned that she had written the name there so she'd remember to pray for that family. What a great idea! I'm sure that Carol saw those letters on her hand many times throughout that day and sent little sentence-long prayers up for them. When God said we are engraved on the palms of His hands, it means that we *cannot* slip out of His awareness. Aha! There it is again—*attention.* God's attention is *always* on you . . . on me. We *never* slip out of His awareness! To reestablish intimacy with Him, then, we need to increase our attentiveness to Him. (In the latter part of this chapter, I'll offer some suggestions for putting this into practice.)

We could think of our relationship with God as being like electricity. The power in an electrical outlet is always available, waiting only for something to be plugged into it so that it can be released. God's love is always waiting for us to plug into it. Our attention focused on Him is the plug-in that connects us, and the life-transforming force of that connection carries with it echoes of creation itself.

Depending on Our Ultimate Friend

Can you imagine what it would be like to live constantly in a state of absolute love, and then willingly to pass from that into all the pain, suffering, and ugliness of a sinful world? I believe that Christ's sacrifice of being born into the world is almost as great as the sacrifice of His death! There is much joy to be found on earth, but let's admit it—life also hurts a lot. Temptation and rejection, humiliation, betrayal, excruciating pain: our Lord knew that all of these awaited Him, and yet He was so drawn by His own love for you and me that He was willing to become human like us. What unspeakable love there is in that! Out of love, Christ took on human form, to be born of a woman, in a lowly place. And why? For what purpose? Hear the words of Robert Fowkes, who helped to form my spiritual life when I was a child:

> Up to the time of the crucifixion, human beings knew themselves to be outcasts and sinners before the absolute goodness of God. They could cry out in sorrow at their own transgressions, but the evil did not vanish with the cry. The sin remained, an eternal demerit. They offered God burnt offerings and blood of lambs, but when they got through, their sins were still with them. But Jesus was the perfect lamb. He owed no price for guilt, and therefore was free to assume the guilt of others as a sacrifice. And He was God, a part of the Holy Trinity. Where man had not the wherewithal to pay the debt, the One to whom it was owed was the only One who could pay. Man had to die on the cross; God had to die on the cross. The debtor, and the One to Whom the debt was owed became one. Death became the source of life—life eternal.[2]

Because Jesus took us all on as *family,* we are His adopted brothers and sisters . . . and we are even more. He also called us by a name that denotes love in one of its deepest meanings: *friend.* "No longer do I call you servants . . . but I have called you friends" (John 15:15, RSV).

Most problems in human relationships, I think, can be reduced to the common denominator of fear of abandonment on one side or the other, even though we often fail to realize that fear or find it hard to admit. It was during a time of great loneliness in my life that I came to know Jesus as my best Friend and to discover the steadfastness of my unleaving Companion. Because of certain childhood experiences, I have sometimes been afraid to let myself get very close to individuals I might otherwise have cared very deeply about. And yet it was during a time when I felt abandoned by someone I loved that I began to realize, in some deep part of myself, that I was not alone. With just the least opening of my self, my friend Jesus made me aware of His intimate presence; and I came to know, absolutely and without the least doubt, the truth of Paul's words in Romans 8:35–39 (RSV):

> Who shall separate us from the love of Christ? Shall tribulation, or distress, or persecution, or famine, or nakedness, or peril, or sword? . . . No, in all these things we are more than conquerors through him who loved us. For I am sure that neither death, nor life, nor angels, nor principalities, nor things present, nor things to come, nor powers, nor height, nor depth, nor anything else in all creation, will be able to separate us from the love of God in Christ Jesus our Lord.

It is in the exercise of that relationship of *friend to friend* that Jesus' love touches us most intimately and profoundly: "Greater love has no man than this, that a man lay down his life for his friends" (John 15:13, RSV).

Living with the Indwelling Spirit

We can relate to God the Father because the human father-child relationship gives us a frame of reference. The same is true with God the Son. But it may be more difficult to think of intimacy with God the Holy Spirit, because "spirit" is such an intangible thing. As a young woman who had lost her husband to cancer put it, "The Holy Spirit is so untouchable. Sometimes I just wish my God were not so *invisible!*" Perhaps the only way we can really talk about the Holy Spirit is through metaphor. And perhaps the only way we can know that He truly exists is by our own personal relationship with Him and by seeing the fruits of His presence in others.

I have seen lives marvelously changed when people have become deeply aware of the fact that the Holy Spirit dwells within them. A woman I've known for years went into a long siege of depression following a major surgery. In addition to this, she'd had a lifelong problem with stuttering. Her depression was so crippling that for months the only thing she could do was to read, so she started reading her Bible. Day after day she read and studied it, until the cover fell off and the pages, almost in shreds, began falling out. As she read and prayed, she discovered the Holy Spirit.

"How did you find Him in the Bible?" I asked her.

"Well," she answered, "it's not that He is on the pages. It's not even the fact that the words in it are living things, although they are. No, it's something more. It was only when I let go and just let the words and all they represent enter into me that I became aware that the Holy Spirit actually dwells within me, loving me, guiding me, even praying within me!"

This woman is now healthy, both physically and emotionally, and her speech problem has disappeared. She leads a Bible study and speaks to various other groups of people in a very fluent, articulate manner. When she tells me that she has personally experienced the love of the Holy Spirit, I believe her because of the changes I see in her life.

Ken Wilbur, author of *Eye to Eye,* asserts that there are three ways by which individuals make contact with reality. They are: the eye of the flesh (physical senses); the eye of reason (the intellect); and the eye of contemplation (spiritual intuition).[3] It is during contemplation—quiet listening, just being present with God, or (as some of the young people I know like to put it) just "hanging out with God"—that we come into most direct contact with the Holy Spirit. That reality and His presence are every bit as real as the chair you're sitting in, as real as the dearest, most beloved person in your life. If you feel you haven't truly experienced the

presence of the Holy Spirit in your life, perhaps you need to
spend more of your prayer time simply listening within. It
is well worth whatever effort it takes to arrange for the
privacy and time alone with Him that it requires. Paul Brunton writes:

> Once we push the gate of the soul slightly ajar and let
> the light stream in, the meaning of life becomes silently
> revealed to us. The gate may be open for one minute or
> for one hour, but in that period we discover the secret
> and neither weary time nor bitter woe can tear that
> priceless knowledge away from us. . . .[4]

I have known the truth of this in my own life. Because of
those wondrous moments when I have felt the breath of the
Holy Spirit on me, I have come to absolutely *know,* deep in
my heart, that the Light dwells within me (John 1:9). It's
very important to make clear the fact that this does not mean
that all of my problems have evaporated, or that I have all
the answers, or that I've "got it all together." Those who
know me best can tell you that is not true. What it does mean
to me is that, in spite of my own sinfulness, regardless of my
weaknesses, even in the midst of the greatest stresses and
storms of my life, *I have an inner anchor* in the Holy Spirit.

The Holy Spirit also provides guidance, just as Jesus said
He would: "When the Spirit of truth comes, he will guide you
into all the truth" (John 16:13, RSV). He is, in fact, the source
of our highest and best direction because He is in touch with
all that is, and can therefore make the connections that are
best for each of us in any given situation. In other words, at
every moment, He dwells within us, *knowing.* That is the
grace, the free gift. Our part is to become still enough within
to sense His leadings and then to *follow* those nudgings. This
last part is extremely important, for the more faithful we can
be in carrying out His directions, the more He will be able
to reveal God's will to us.

Haven't we all had those times when we've prayed about
something and dismissed it from our minds and then later
found ourselves participating in the answer to our prayer?
Here's a personal example.

Several years ago, when my son Paul was in a serious car
accident, we needed a witness to prove that he hadn't been

speeding; but as far as we knew, no one had seen the accident. For many nights I prayed about the situation. Then I let go of it and got occupied with taking care of Paul, who had been critically injured in the accident.

About a week before the hearing was scheduled, I started thinking about a friend I hadn't seen for a long time. I felt a little guilty because I had not called her for so long, even though I knew she was lonely. But I kept pushing the thought out of my mind, because of the upcoming hearing and all the other things going on at the time. Still, I couldn't seem to get Joline out of my thoughts. Finally, I decided just to give her a quick phone call to let her know I hadn't forgotten her. In the course of the conversation, I mentioned the court hearing.

"But Paul wasn't speeding," Joline said.

"How do you know?" I asked.

"My daughter Carol said they talked about it in history class and Rocky [a classmate] said that he was right behind Paul's car when it went off the road, that he'd been following him for several blocks, and that they were both going about twenty miles per hour."

Suddenly, I knew why I'd had that insistent urge to call Joline. Thank God I responded to it! Paul's name was cleared.

I know that you have had similar experiences. I do not believe that such events are coincidences. I like the statement I heard recently at a retreat: "There are no coincidences, only God-incidents." I believe that such events in the life of a praying person are evidences of the living love of the Holy Spirit and of His active participation in our lives. They are also builders of intimacy with God.[5]

One of the ways the Bible adds facets to my concept of the Holy Spirit is by comparing Him with familiar things, such as wind, a dove, and living water. These models have added wonderful depths to my awareness of the love that is of the Spirit. For instance, in the Hebrew of the Old Testament and the Greek of the New Testament, the word that is used for *spirit* is the same word that is used for *wind* and for *breath.* In John 3:8, Jesus directly compares the movements of the Holy Spirit to the wind. Having lived in Nebraska all of my life, I know about wind! Among the many parallels is the fact that wind, though invisible, can be known by its effect on things that *are* visible. It's the same with the Holy Spirit. He can be known by the effects He has upon the lives of those who have developed a relationship with Him. "The fruit of the Spirit is love, joy, peace, long-suffering, gentleness, goodness, faith, meekness, temperance" (Galatians 5:22). Wind also provides *lift* for kites, airplanes, birds, and the human spirit.

Even more revealing, I think, is the parallel between Spirit and breath. From the moment of birth until the moment of death, breath is part of us, continually providing what we need from outside of ourselves and then, as it's exhaled, carrying away those elements that we are ready to release. The connection between Spirit and breath helps me to sense the gift of my intimacy with the Holy Spirit.

As a means of awareness, you might want to try something that I've found helpful in opening myself to Him. Close your eyes, and, as you take a long, slow, deep breath, remind yourself that you are symbolically breathing in Spirit. Hold the breath for just long enough to say in your heart, "I am filled with the Holy Spirit." Then, as you exhale, breathe out all negativity (such as anger, tension, resentment). Just release it all. Then inhale Spirit again, feeling yourself filled with Him. Continue in this way for five breaths, and I think you'll be richly blessed with a greater awareness of the fact that "closer is He than breathing, and nearer than hands and feet."[6] At various times throughout the day, you can renew your awareness of your connection with the Holy Spirit by taking a deep breath or two while being mindful of the tie between breath and Spirit. It's a builder of intimacy.

The second metaphor that helps me to know the Holy Spirit is the image of the dove. I recently read something interesting about the reason why God chose the dove as the symbol for the Holy Spirit.[7] (See John 1:32, in which the Spirit descends upon Jesus *like a dove.*) It relates to the passage in Romans: "We do not know what we ought to pray, but the Spirit himself intercedes for us with groans that words cannot express" (8:26, NIV). Doves moan. They really do. They make an almost constant sound, like a holy chant. Yes! The Holy Spirit is like a dove, descending to us on frail white wings of prayer, constantly uttering intercessions for you and me in ways we can't begin to understand. What an *intimacy of love* there is in that, a grace that soars on the wings of the wind.

In Gerard Manley Hopkins' beautiful poem "God's Grandeur," he writes of how human beings have trodden down and smudged and smeared God's lovely creation. But then the poet continues:

And for all this, nature is never spent;
There lives the dearest freshness deep down things;
And though the last lights off the black West went
Oh, morning, at the brown brink eastward, springs—
Because the Holy Ghost over the bent
World broods with warm breast and with ah! bright
   wings.[8]

How blessed we are to know that we are loved by the one God who is Father, Son, and Holy Spirit—Creator, Redeemer, Comforter. The more fully we can learn to trust that love, the more desirous we will be of spending time with our God. And the more time we spend with Him, the deeper will be our awareness of His love. It's an upward spiral that has no limit.

The Hole at the Center

Yet, though we know God loves us, we sometimes still feel empty. I believe that much of the pain in our lives grows out of the fact that God created us for intimacy with Him, but that we have fallen away from that. We feel the terrible emptiness that results, but we try to fill it with all the wrong things.

Columnist Bernard Levin wrote: "There is a hole inside of most people, and no matter how much food and drink they pour into it, however many cars and TV sets they stuff it with, however many well-balanced children and loyal friends they parade around the edges of it . . . it aches."[9]

There have been times in my life when I've felt lonely because I've wanted to be close to someone but have only been able to connect with them in a superficial way. Perhaps you've experienced that, too. When it's happened to me, I've sensed that there is some hungry part of me waiting, like a gaping baby bird, alone and unfed.

Here is what my own "hole at the center" has taught me: God Himself placed that ache within me . . . in the hope that it would draw me to Him. Only He can fill it in a way that will nourish and satisfy my deepest longings. Like the Psalmist, I have come to know that "my soul thirsteth for thee, my flesh longeth for thee in a dry and thirsty land, where no water is" (Psalm 63:1). I have also had to accept the fact that the longing will never be fully satisfied during this lifetime. That's the way it's meant to be, in order to keep drawing us back to Him.

A woman I'll call Lucy told me about her struggles with the hole at the center of her. She and John were married in their late teens, after a short courtship. Soon after that, they began having children (six of them in all). John worked for the railroad and so was away from home quite a bit, but Lucy was busy with the children and exhausted by the end of the day, so she didn't notice that her spirit was crying out for intimacy. When her youngest child started to school, Lucy began to develop her musical talents. In addition to playing the piano, she loved to sing, so she joined the church choir. Before long, she found herself responding to the attentions of a very attractive young tenor. For a while, the hole inside of her felt filled. But there was a constant fight within her, because she felt guilty about her feelings and knew she could never act on them. Every week, she went home from choir practice feeling more and more lonely. Gradually, the romance wore off, and Lucy found herself in a deep depression. Before long, though, a man in a couples' group she and John belonged to started calling Lucy from his office during the day. She came right up out of her depression, and life seemed wonderful again for a while. But that relationship, too, failed to satisfy.

Over and over again, Lucy kept falling in love, and every time, she asked herself, "What's wrong with me?" When she found herself in love with her sister's husband, she was suddenly jolted awake to the fact that no human relationship, however uplifting, however exciting, would ever be the answer to her problem. It was unrealistic for her to expect John to satisfy all of her needs for intimacy, but it was also impossible for any other person to make her feel whole. Lucy went to her pastor, who suggested a daily program of spiritual disciplines. At first, she had to force herself to practice the prayer and Bible reading he recommended, but gradually, in very subtle ways, she began to feel a change within her. She started looking forward to her time with God. As she followed her pastor's suggestion to read and meditate on the Song of Solomon daily for an entire month, she began to sense that her true beloved is God, and her need for other men diminished.

Lucy tells me that she still enjoys male attention but it's not a threat to her marriage or to her spirit any more, because she knows, now, that only God can fill the empty spaces in her.

Even though God created us for intimacy with Him, we keep falling away from it. There is no way that we can feel intimate with Him at all times. When we don't, we simply have to act on the knowledge that is set down for us in the Bible, trusting that God has not moved away from us. At a retreat, a lady named Fran told me that as her husband was driving her to work one day, she noticed a couple in the car ahead. The girl's head rested on the boy's shoulder. Suddenly nostalgic, Fran turned to her husband and said, "How come we never sit close like that any more?" Dan looked at the space between Fran and him and then replied, "*I* haven't moved!"

Alienation from God is always caused by us, not by Him. He does not move away from us. How, then, can we move closer to Him?

Making Time for a Friend

There are several very practical things we can do to increase our intimacy with God. It's quite a bit like building a friendship.

When my friend Jan moved to town, each of us sensed in a deep way that God had sent the other to be her friend. We'd both been praying for just such a spiritual sister. The first thing we decided to do was to get together for an hour or so every weekday, in order to get to know each other. I'd never done that before! I saw most of my other friends about once a week, some no more than once a month. I always intended to plan something with them "just as soon as I get caught up." Well, as you know, that time never comes; so I didn't really have a truly intimate relationship with anyone outside of my family. But since Jan and I *scheduled* our time together, we found that in just a very short time we got past the small-talk stage and began to share the deeper, more important parts of who we are. I wouldn't have thought I'd have time for a daily talk, but I was surprised to discover that I did. Maybe it was because I wanted the friendship so much.

Intimacy with God develops in the same way . . . a little at a time, through daily companionship. It happens when you really *want it enough to schedule time for it,* the way you would a daily class or appointment.

If you've had trouble sticking to a daily prayer time, maybe it's because you're trying to have your appointment with God during a time you're at a low ebb physically. For years, I tried to have my quiet time with God the first thing in the morning, before breakfast. But I just couldn't keep my mind on Him. It kept wandering away into thoughts about the upcoming day or a dream of the night, or just lapsing back into a state of half-sleep. Sometimes my stomach growled and all I could think about was toast and coffee.

Now I keep a little prayer card on my bedside table and I pray that short prayer each morning.[10] Even though I've memorized it, I read it aloud from the card. It's the only way I can keep my mind from wandering off that early in the morning. But I have scheduled a half hour to an hour of time with God at ten o'clock in the evening. I'm a night person and that just works better for me.

So think about it. When, during your nonworking hours, are you most alert? Plan to give God some of your *best* time, instead of offering Him the time when you're not quite all there! Then write it on your daily calendar pad, or your list of "Things to Do Today." Consider it an appointment that must not be broken.

Maybe a half hour to an hour seems too long for you. There have been times when I've felt that way. But now it seems to be not long enough. I think it's because I've learned to be more honest before God. I talk to Him about all of the junk of the day, including the parts that hurt. Again, it's like friendship. As you get to know another person, your level of trust begins to get stronger, so that you can share not only the daily incidents but also your deep feelings. You can begin to talk about the things that hurt, or the mistakes you've made, as well as your greatest joys.

Early in our friendship, I told Jan something I felt guilty about. It just spilled out, and I could hardly believe I'd said that to her! But she was very accepting and thanked me for being honest with her, and it brought us closer. We'll come back to the subject of human intimacy in chapter 5, but my reason for bringing it in at this point is that I've seen that there's something about admitting my failings to God that gives me the same kind of closeness. It seems to me that the Hebrew people of the Old Testament had that kind of honesty before God. Abraham, Isaac, Jacob, Moses, David—all of them expressed anger toward God, and they complained to Him and admitted their own failings. It would be impossible to read the Psalms without sensing this same honesty. That's why it helps me to include at least one Psalm in my daily prayer time. It reminds me to get my own garbage out. I know that God can handle it, even when I can't.

I have to admit that I'm not always faithful to my daily prayer time, but I'm trying very hard to keep it. On those days when I'm really swamped or exhausted, I've found that shortening my prayer time, instead of skipping it altogether, helps to keep me faithful.

Daily prayer is the first requirement for intimacy with God. Beyond that, I've found wonderful nurturing for that Number One relationship by arranging for longer periods of alone time, when I can. Every few months, I try to spend twenty-four hours alone with God in the little hermitage cottage at a monastery not far from our town. Often, when I get there, I'm feeling heavy with personal problems, tired from too much busyness, or just separated from God in some way. I arrive in the evening, and as the dusk turns to darkness, I light the little kerosene lantern that sits on the desk, open my spiral notebook, and begin to write a letter to God. I tell Him all the ways I can think of that I've strayed away from Him. As honestly as I can, I write down all the guilty thoughts I've been carrying around with me. I know that sounds as if it would feel terrible, but no! It's just the opposite. It's absolutely *restoring* to get all that off my chest! It's like cleaning the inside of the cup. Jesus said we should first clean what's inside, and the cleansing of the outer part of the cup (soul) will follow (Matthew 23:26). So, after writing all of that down, I ask His forgiveness and destroy the written pages. It's as if Jesus has said to me personally, as He did to so many others when He walked on earth: "Be of good cheer; thy sins be forgiven thee" (Matthew 9:2). In that time of honesty before God, the walls that my sins have built crumble into dust, and I know, once again, that I am called *friend*.

Of course, you don't need a cottage in which to do this, but you do need some time alone in a private place so that you can "be still, and know that I am God" (Psalm 46:10). It doesn't have to be twenty-four hours. If you can only arrange a half hour, take *that* as His gift and offer it back to Him. He may magnify and increase it! I have found that time is actually rather elastic when I'm in intimate relationship with God. Here's something I think is exciting: no matter how busy I am, if I'm willing to give Him even a smidgen of time, He will take that gift and use it to open up *more* time for developing my friendship with Him. It's not only loaves and fishes that He knows how to multiply!

Trusting the Net

Next to spending time with God, the most important factor that leads to intimacy with Him is acknowledging our dependency on Him.

I once had a dream in which I was walking on a tightrope between two skyscrapers. Suddenly, the rope broke; as I started to fall, I grabbed the broken ends and hung there, feet dangling over the street, suspended in the air. I was sure that if I let go of either rope, I'd fall to my death. I can still feel the terror of that. And yet, at the same time, I knew that my only hope was in *letting myself fall*. With a pounding heart, I closed my eyes and let go of the ropes. I fell . . . and fell . . . and fell . . . and then, just as I expected to hit the sidewalk . . .

I bounced! There had been an *invisible net* under me all along! As I rebounded into the air, I was amazed to find that I was soaring like a bird!

I've thought about that dream many times since. For me, it has become a symbol of dying into life. And I've come to know that there *is* an invisible net under me—a spiritual net that connects me with God, with my truest self, and with others. God's grace is already within, above, around, and underneath you and me, but we can't really know that for sure until we let go, until we can say to Him, "I give up, Lord. You take over." Then, amazingly, we discover the invisible net of God's sure presence. It has been there all along, waiting to save us, to help us to rebound, to give us the mental, emotional, and spiritual lift that we need.

Living the Gift

How can we claim the priceless gift of intimacy with God? Let's resolve to:

- Let down our barriers, be flat-out honest with God.
- Remember that we get more of what we focus our attention on. Focus on Him.
- When we're troubled or hurting, remind ourselves that we are engraved on the palm of His hand.
- Think of Jesus as our Friend, the One who loves us with all our faults and will never abandon us.
- Soak ourselves in Scripture until we know that the Holy Spirit has taken up residence within us. Then soak some more!
- Let metaphors, such as the wind, a dove, and living water make the Spirit more real to us.
- When we feel a lonely ache, remember that it's God calling us to Him.
- Schedule time for Him daily.
- Acknowledge our dependency on Him.
- Learn and practice spiritual disciplines.[11]

Ralph Waldo Emerson wrote, "Into every intelligence there is a door through which the Creator passes." Oh yes!

It is true. Let us open ourselves to the best of all possible friendships by claiming the gift of intimacy with God.[12]

NOTES

1. Stephen Gaskin, *This Season's People* (Summertown, Tenn.: Book Publishing Company, 1976).

2. The Reverend Francis Fowkes, from an unpublished Lenten meditation.

3. Ken Wilbur, "The Problem of Proof," *ReVision,* volume 5, no. 1 (Spring, 1982): pp. 80–100. Wilbur is using the terminology of the Christian philosopher and teacher, St. Bonaventure.

4. Paul Brunton, *The Secret Path,* as cited by Willis Harman and Howard Rheingold in *Higher Creativity* (Los Angeles: J. P. Tarcher, 1984), p. 80.

5. The question arises, How do we know whether or not the guidance is from the Holy Spirit? Couldn't it be just our own mind playing tricks on us, or our unconscious rationalizing to get *our* way? Of course that's very possible, and it's a valid question. In the book *The Graces of Interior Prayer,* A. G. Poulin suggests three criteria by which we should test the validity of inner guidance: First, "Does the insight lead to virtuous conduct, to feelings of deep and lasting satisfaction, to a sense of joy, peace, and love, or to actions which seem to produce good results?" Second, "Does it check with the similar experiences of others (in other words, with tradition)?" This criterion is often misunderstood. It does not mean that tradition is right and unchanging. It does mean that the historical experience of others should not be ignored. Finally, "Is it accompanied and followed by a noetic sense of profound truth that persists long after the experience is over?" (Cited by Harman and Rheingold, *Higher Creativity,* p. 125.)

6. Alfred Lord Tennyson, "The Higher Pantheism."

7. Letter from Carl P. Daw to Ray Glover, October 15, 1986, in the Church Hymnal Corporation Papers, New

York, N.Y., about the hymn by Carl P. Daw, "Like the Murmur of the Dove's Song." Quoted in Ray Glover, *Commentary on New Hymns* (New York: Church Pension Fund, 1987).

8. Gerard Manley Hopkins, "God's Grandeur," in *Poems and Prose of Gerard Manley Hopkins,* ed. W. H. Gardner (Baltimore: Penguin Books, 1963), p. 27.

9. Bernard Levin, *The London Times,* 1978.

10. The first-thing-in-the-morning prayer I use most often is by Marilyn Norquist: *"Father, I don't know what is going to happen today or how I will handle whatever comes up. But I know I'm dependent on you, and I trust you in every situation. Even though I may forget at the moment, I tell you now that I want your guidance, to fulfill your purpose for each circumstance.* Amen."

11. Among the spiritual practices that have helped me in my ongoing efforts to become more intimate with God are: the Jesus Prayer, which I'll describe in chapter 7, journaling, praying with Scripture, prayer walks, praying aloud when alone, and praying the Psalms. Since I have written about these prayer forms in my previous books, I'll not repeat my discussion of them here. See especially *A Guide to Christian Meditation* (New York: Walker and Co., 1980); *Where Soul and Spirit Meet* (Nashville: Abingdon Press, 1986); and *God's Best for You* (New York: Macmillan, 1988).

12. Ralph Waldo Emerson, *On Man and God* (Mount Vernon, N.Y.: Peter Pauper Press, 1961), p. 15.

CHAPTER 5

The Gift of Connecting with Others

"A new commandment I give to you, that you love one another; even as I have loved you, that you also love one another."

John 13:34, RSV

Several years ago, I came across a beautiful poem by Lesley and Earl Barfoot that expressed one of the deepest desires of my heart—the longing for true intimacy. Again and again I have gone back to those words, holding them as a model, a hope, and a prayer. I'd like to share the Barfoots' poem with you because I think it captures the essence of the truly intimate relationship.

> Walk with me through the places
> Of deepest truth,
> That my life and yours
> May touch each other
> In blessing.
>
> Let us explore, together,
> Those mysteries of essential being
> With which God has endowed us,
> That we may know each other
> With wonder.

May we offer to each other,
In celebration, that unconditional love
Which is an extension of God's love
Moving freely through us
To fulfill each other.

Then we shall know
The touch of God upon our lives,
Making beautiful the experience
Of being human,
Giving fleeting moments
Eternal dimension,
That we may be for each other
Symbols of the sacred.[1]

To be "symbols of the sacred" for each other: perhaps that's intimacy at its best. Isn't that what God meant us to be for each other when He said, "It is not good that the man should be alone" (Genesis 2:18, RSV)?

Being Symbols of the Sacred

As I think back on my life, certain people stand out as my symbols of the sacred—my father, my Aunt Alta, Father Robert Fowkes (the minister of my teen years) . . . and my best high school friend, Jeri Howard.

Jeri was the first person with whom I really shared my deepest beliefs. Often, on summer evenings, she and I would sit on the curb halfway between her house and mine, or under the cherry tree in my back yard, listening to the sounds of cicadas in the trees around us, breathing rain-fresh air, and just talking quietly. Sometimes we shared our doubts. Often we talked about the big questions of life, such as why we are here, how each of us experienced God, what prayer means. But just as often, we shared the little daily moments that kept waking us up to God's presence with us in the world.

Once, Jeri told me about climbing up onto her father's lap because she was lonely for her brother who had gone away to join the navy. We talked about the fact that God is like a father, with His arms and lap always available, waiting to comfort us when we're hurting. It's an image I still turn to when I'm lonely or sad. Another time Jeri brought me a

picture of a lighthouse that she'd cut out of a magazine, and
we talked about Christ's light being in each of us, and that
we need to keep shining to light each other's way. We shared
favorite Bible passages and talked about what they meant.
We discovered that our ways of seeing were not always the
same, but somehow we came to know that was okay.

As our friendship grew, we admitted to each other our
most closely guarded secrets—about the things we'd done we
were ashamed of, about our undeclared love for a couple of
boys who probably didn't know we existed, about our problems with our stuffy old parents. Sometimes Jeri and I got
very angry with each other, and for a few days we'd hardly
speak; but always, the bond between us kept drawing us back
to each other. It just seemed that there was a wonderful,
invisible connection that grew out of those quiet talks, a
connection that has never been broken, even though Jeri lives
in California and I in Nebraska.

One day recently, during my prayer time, Jeri kept coming
to my mind. Since I haven't seen her for years and we don't
write very regularly, that was an unusual thing, so I felt God
wanted me to pray for her. Afterwards, I wrote her a short
note, telling her what had happened. About a week later, I
received a beautiful letter from her, telling me that on the day
I was led to pray for her, she had had a test for cancer, and
that she'd had a great amount of anxiety. The test did come
back negative, but that's not the real point of my telling you
this. It's an illustration of my solid belief that true spiritual
intimacy is beyond time and space. My friendship with Jeri
was my first taste of real intimacy.

Discovering the Priceless Treasure

The need for intimacy, for closeness, is one of the deepest
needs of every human being. It is magnetic in the sense that,
like the God-hole we talked about in the last chapter, it keeps
trying to draw us in the direction of a priceless treasure. Yet
many of us live our whole lifetime without ever finding
the holy grail of true intimacy with others, not because we
haven't met the right people, but because we haven't understood our own *connecting needs.*

To know that at least one other person honestly cares about what happens to us is as real a need as hunger or thirst. Down deep we long for the sense of validity that comes from knowing someone has truly *heard* us, even if they don't agree with what we've said. We need to be able to let down our barricades and boundaries enough to allow another to see the real person inside of us, and not just the masks we wear.

When we are admired for our achievements, our beauty, our intelligence, money, athletic ability, sense of humor, or artistic talent, some deep part of us knows that it is only our outer shell that is loved, not our real self. We need to know that there is someone who would love us even if they knew all our secret sins, hateful feelings, unholy thoughts, weaknesses, failures, and painful memories. We desperately want to connect with another, true-self to true-self. And it *is* possible, even though such closeness does not mean we'll always be in harmony or that there will never be any problems in our relationship. What it does mean is that when that authentic connection is made, we know we have touched something holy, a genuine *grace,* precious beyond words.

By Revealing Ourselves

Intimacy comes when two people reach over the tops of their own invisible walls of self-protection and clasp hands. Then, gradually, brick by brick, they risk letting the other person see more and more of who they really are. Each time we share a dream, admit a fear, or reveal a memory, we remove a brick of the wall. As we share—and keep—confidences, our trust builds and we gain courage to reveal more of ourselves. Though the wall will never be completely eliminated (and shouldn't be), intimacy risks exposure for the sake of touching on a deeper level. It can be scary, but how great are the rewards! To feel that you are truly *known* by another human being is to know that you are not, and never again will be, alone in the world. Being known by another person, we are better able to know ourselves.

Intimacy is not clinging or possessiveness. Rather, it is two people standing together, touching emotionally and spiritually, sometimes physically if appropriate, and letting go, free to move together or separately, each knowing that the other person will be there for them when they need a listening ear, a gentle prod, or someone to say, "Here, let me carry that heavy load for half an hour." I love to watch the paired figure-skating performances during the winter Olympics, because they create for me a good picture of an intimate relationship. The skaters sometimes move along side by side; sometimes they come together and move in delightful unison; then they move apart, soloing with grace and controlled freedom, coming together again when it's right. The beauty of the ice dance includes movements in which one skater lifts or carries the other, which means one skater must be willing to be lifted or carried by the other. All of this is part of what it means to be intimate.

Turning Each Other to God

For me, the best intimacy always has a spiritual focus. We do not become God to each other, but we keep turning each other toward God.

Sometimes God's timing absolutely stuns me. If I hadn't lived what I'm about to tell you, I wouldn't believe it, but it is true. Just this morning, as I sat here thinking of how to illustrate this fact about spiritual intimacy, the phone rang. It was a longtime friend whom I haven't seen or talked with in over two months. She called, she said, just to ask how I'm doing. Well, the truth is that I've been feeling very weak and emotionally drained because of the many things I must do during the upcoming weeks, some of them emotionally charged and stressful. When I told Dorothy I was feeling somewhat overwhelmed, she said that must have been why thoughts of me kept coming to her during her prayer time.

Dorothy and I have shared spiritually, though sporadically, for many years, sometimes touching on a deep level, often strongly disagreeing, but almost always ending our conversations or visits by praying together. Today, she simply said, "Just remember that God is on your side." Now that was a very simple statement, but it turned me away from my worry about the outcome of an unsettling situation and brought my focus back to God. To me, that's what spiritual intimacy is all about.

By Accepting God's Value of Us

With intimacy, as with every grace, God is always waiting to give us more than we ask. But surprisingly, we often sabotage our own chances for closeness!

By far the greatest barrier to loving others is our inability to truly value ourselves. If I'm afraid that, deep down, I'm a bad person or an unlovable person, the last thing I'll dare to do is to let you get to know the real me. So I'll present a false self to you, hoping to fool you into liking me. Of course, it doesn't work, because if you end up liking the person I pretend to be, somewhere inside the real me sits lonely and crying, like a lost and orphaned child.

At a recent Christian-living seminar, we talked about the need to get to know ourselves better. A frail young woman in a gray dress, who hadn't spoken a word during the weekend, said, "But what if you really just don't like yourself very well? Why would you want to get to know yourself better, if you already know that you're not a very likable person?"

I think there are times when all of us feel that way, but there is a most amazing answer to that young lady's question. It's true, of course, that there are things within ourselves that are unlovable, and those darknesses need to be looked at and then offered to Christ. But underneath all of that, there *is* a beautiful, lovable person in you. That beauty has always been there and always will be. It is the very *essence of you*. It is the person God created, before all of the negative programming started layering itself over the spirit of you. *Your very nature is light.* In John 1:9, we learn that Christ Himself lights *every person* who comes into the world. No matter how sinful you have been, no matter how filled with self-loathing you might now be, that Christ light is still shining in you, and in becoming intimate with God and with yourself, you will discover it. Then you can begin to let go of all that is unlovely in you, and your inner glow will begin to radiate outward, drawing others to you.

By Loving Ourselves

In the dream I told about in the last chapter, I was suspended precariously between two skyscrapers and had to let myself fall in order to be saved. I discovered that there was an invisible net under me: a symbol of my connection with God, with myself, and with others. The net of connecting is *always triangular.* Intimacy with others, the third corner of the net, depends on (1) intimacy with God (John 13:34) and (2) intimacy with self—"Thou shalt love thy neighbor as thyself" (Matthew 19:19). Only when these two connections are solid can we truly relate to others in a loving way. Many relationships fail because they are not held up by a spiritual connection coupled with the solid interlacings of self-knowledge. Let's see how intimacy with self can help us find closeness with others.

Loving yourself is not the same thing as being selfish. Any time the word *self* is used, it tends to conjure up old parental warnings, such as, "Now, stop being so selfish and share your toys." I think many of us were brought up with the spoken or unspoken message that anything we do for ourselves is selfish. This can be a huge stumbling-block, which often causes us to try to meet everybody else's needs, while neglecting our own. Of course, this doesn't work because it leads to swallowed resentment and burnout, and eventually we have very little left to give.

I still cringe a little when someone says, "Well, I have to take care of my own needs first." Yet I'm beginning to see that many of those people are also the ones who have active, intimate relationships, and are reaching out to others in honest, authentic ways, from the solid base of knowing who they really are.

I'm not advocating selfishness or "me-first-ism." It's just that I know that God wants us to love ourselves. Jesus reduced the law to two commandments: "Thou shalt love the Lord thy God with all thy heart, and with all thy soul, and with all thy mind. . . . [and] thy neighbor *as thyself*" (Matthew 22:37, 39, italics mine). Clearly, our Lord's two commandments include a taken-for-granted third requirement— that we love ourselves. So, again, there's that three-way net upon which true intimacy rests: love of God, self, and others.

The times in my own life when I've felt most alone have been those times when I've neglected my relationship with my inner self, when all of my focus has been on external things, when I've been so caught up in *doing* that I've failed to take time for *being.* When that happens, my soul and spirit seem to shrivel up, and I find that my feelings are easily hurt, or I start having trouble trusting people, or I say things I don't mean. I need to realize, when this occurs, that the other people are not the problem. I'm the one who's causing the trouble, because I've neglected my intimate relationship with myself.

Dr. Jerry Greenwald, psychotherapist and author of the book *Creative Intimacy* writes: "Intimacy with oneself is basic to all intimate relating with others."[2] Think about the people you know. Aren't you drawn most to those who clearly like themselves? People who go around saying (either by word or by action), "I'm a failure. No one likes me. Poor me," create a negative atmosphere around themselves that makes others want to avoid them. I have found that, to a considerable extent, *people tend to accept our own evaluation of ourselves.*

Learning to Know Ourselves

You may have your own ways of reconnecting with your intimate self, but here are some things that have helped me when I've felt alienated from who I am inside.

Journaling

One of the most valuable enhancers of self-intimacy for me is journaling. Talking to yourself is sometimes a sign of insanity, but I also believe that *not* talking to yourself can make you mentally ill! The way I talk to myself is by writing down my thoughts and, especially, my feelings in a notebook, trying very hard not to hold back anything. There's no need to, since I'm only talking to me, anyway. There are things I can say in my journal that I couldn't possibly say to my family or my best friend. If you decide to try this, write as if you were talking to the one person in all the world who truly understands you and who will not hold anything against you. Go ahead and *rage,* if that's what you're feeling, or pour out your self-pity, or express your fears and anxieties and despair, even your anger at God. The psalmists knew the value in this. For example:

> Have mercy upon me, O Lord; for I am weak: O Lord,
> heal me; for my bones are vexed. My soul is also sore
> vexed: but thou, O Lord, how long? . . . I am weary with
> my groaning; all the night make I my bed to swim; I
> water my couch with my tears.
>
> *Psalm 6:2–3, 6*

> My God, my God, why hast thou forsaken me? why art
> thou so far from helping me, and from the words of my
> roaring? O my God, I cry in the daytime, but thou
> hearest not; and in the night season, and am not silent.
>
> *Psalm 22:1–2*

Just get it all out, both the joys and the sorrows of each day.
Then (and this is absolutely essential) offer it all to God,
ending your journal entry with praise and thanksgiving.

Being Your Own Partner in a Difficult Task

Depending only on myself to accomplish something hard
has helped my self-intimacy to grow, too. My first solo drive
to Colorado, mentioned in a previous chapter, had this effect.
Here's another example.

My brother built a computer for me several years ago,
using a kit. I ordered a word processing program but I had
no one to teach me how to use it. The manuals were quite
technical and difficult to understand at that time, and Don
couldn't help me because he'd never used such a program.
It took me a full two weeks of trial and error, frustration, and
wastebaskets full of ruined paper before I was able to do just
the basic things.

During that time, I hardly saw my family, because I spent
so much time in my office fighting with that machine, which
kept refusing to obey me. There were a couple of times I was
ready to throw the whole electronic mess out my office window, hoping I'd never see it again! But I kept at it. When I
finally completed my first article on the computer and it
printed out right (a miracle), I had the most incredible feeling
of euphoria. The words that went through my head were,
"Hooray! *We* made it!" Then I realized that, all during that
long, difficult, self-learning process, I had not been alone. Of

course, God had been with me, but there was also someone else—someone I felt quite intimate with at that moment—my inner self.

If you decide to try this way of connecting with *you,* choose a task that will take some time, that is difficult but can be accomplished, and assume that you have an ally—your innermost self.

Paying Attention to Your Dreams

Intimacy with the self can also be greatly enhanced by recording your dreams. Even people who think they never dream have found that they can sometimes catch a morning dream just by placing paper and pencil on the bedside table and making a decision to remember what they're dreaming when they first wake up. It may take several days before it happens, but it will happen. I use a spiral notebook, recording the *events* of the dream on the page to the right of the spiral binding. Then I read it over, considering each person or event as symbolic, and writing down my associations with those symbols, and the *feelings* that go with them, on the page to the left of the binding. It's such an "aha!" moment when you discover what your inner self is trying to tell you in a dream.

For example, I recently dreamed that I was getting ready to go to some event but my floor-length dress was too long and I stepped on the hem and couldn't move. I couldn't think of any association with the symbol until I asked myself what was the dominant *feeling* of the dream. It was a sensation of being bound, stuck, unable to move on. Then I realized that the skirt represented a work project that had taken me far too long, symbolized by the pun of the too-long skirt. As I sat reading over what I'd written in my notebook and asking myself what was blocking me, it suddenly occurred to me that it was nothing but my own foot! I was "dragging my feet" (another dream pun) because I was seeing the length of the project as overwhelming. Once I realized that, I decided to change my way of thinking about the work. I could break it down into manageable pieces, set deadlines for myself, and *get moving.*

As soon as I'd written that message to myself in my dream

journal, I felt ten pounds lighter. Much to my delight, the next night I dreamed that I was *waltzing,* in an ankle-length dress! My work has seemed much freer since I've had those dreams. At times, it even seems to dance. Paying attention to that dream put me in touch with my true self and helped me get unstuck.

But what does all of that have to do with developing intimacy with others? Contrary to what one might think, paying attention to the messages from *you* to *you* does *not* foster self-centeredness. In fact, quite the opposite happens. Intimacy with yourself provides a deep reservoir of energy that helps you establish and maintain relationships with others. It gives you a solid base from which to reach out authentically to other people. It also helps you to be less emotionally needy. People who lack self-intimacy tend to look to others to fulfill all of their feeling needs. Those who have a close relationship with their inner person, on the other hand, have an inner strength that others can sense. People feel drawn to them, knowing in some unspoken way that a relationship with that person will be freeing rather than burdening.

Having inner resources to rely on can also help if a relationship ends, for whatever reason. It may still be necessary to grieve the loss, but you have a deep assurance that, after the pain has been worked through, you will be able to reach out again. Knowing that you have at least two allies in the darkness—God as Friend and your intimate self—makes it possible to let go, trusting the net!

Blocking the Flow of Intimacy

In addition to the barrier caused by our failure to love ourselves, we also block out closeness in other ways, such as: by demanding attention; by clinging too tightly; by trying to control others; by placing the responsibility for our own happiness on another person, or by the opposite: making ourselves responsible for someone else's feelings.

In all these ways, we defeat our own purposes by putting so much weight on the tightrope that it finally breaks under the strain.

Demanding Attention

Not long ago, a young woman asked me to pray for healing in her marriage. "I really do love Jim," she insisted, "but I've been feeling more and more unloving lately. I can't figure out what's wrong with me!"

As we talked, Lisa told me how guilty she felt because Jim was always demanding that she give him loving attention. "Lisa! Come rub my back!" Or, "How come you never serve me breakfast in bed anymore?"

"I used to love to do all of those things," Lisa said, "but since he's been demanding them, it isn't fun anymore. I have to force myself to do it. And then, he makes little remarks such as, 'Bill's wife puts love notes in *his* lunch. All *I* get is sandwiches and fruit.'

"I'll tell you one thing," said Lisa, "that may give me the guilties, but it sure doesn't make me feel like writing love notes!"

What Jim didn't realize was that *the more you demand love, the less of it you get.* Loving attention must be freely given. It can't be squeezed out of another person.

Clinging Too Tightly

Perhaps it's a human tendency to think that tightening our hold will keep us close, but of course it has exactly the opposite effect. The more we clutch and cling, the more the other person tries to pull away. There's a line from a play entitled *Claudia,* in which the mother advises her daughter to "hold close with open arms."[3] It's a good bit of wisdom that can improve any relationship, whether between friends, sweethearts, spouses, or parents and children.

For instance, one of the hardest things for us parents to do is to free our children; but only in doing that can we have authentic relationships with them. The process starts so very early. More than anything else in my life, I have wanted to be a good mother. I always believed that, if you just love your children enough, they'll grow up to be happy adults. For me, loving my children included not only taking care of their needs but also giving them plenty of attention and nurturing, and I believe that has been to their good. But at times I went beyond that by trying to protect them from their own feelings. The day I handed my older son Paul over to the motherly looking lady who was to be his preschool teacher two mornings a week, I was suddenly aware of a giant hole, right in the center of my chest. When I turned to leave and my little boy started to cry, it was almost more than I could bear. I gave Mrs. Larson a pleading look and she said, "If a child is having trouble separating, we allow the parent to stay the first morning. Next time, though, it would be better *for him* if you'd just bring him in and then leave quickly."

All through the morning, Paul held onto me with a clutching grip, often burying his head in my shoulder. Several times I tried to put him down, but he just held on tighter and tighter. There were a couple of other mothers having the same problem, so we adults stayed around, trying to get our children involved in the activities, but without success. At the beginning of the day, there had also been two or three children crying because their mothers had left. About midmorning, it suddenly occurred to me that *those* children were now happily playing, participating in the games, relating to the other children, while the ones who were clinging to their mothers were still sidelined!

The next morning, I handed Paul to Mrs. Larson, kissed him good-bye, and went out of the room. Oh. Ouch! My stomach churned and tears welled up in my eyes, as I heard my little boy crying for me. I wanted to go back and say, "It's okay, honey. You don't have to stay. We'll wait till next year." It would have been so much easier. It would also have been a gigantic mistake.

There was an observation window in the next room so that parents and students could watch without the children's being aware of it, so I went in there. For the first few minutes, Paul wouldn't let Mrs. Larson put him down, but before long, she got him interested in putting together a wooden jigsaw puzzle. In a very short time, he let go of her and started talking to a cute little girl with blond pigtails!

Well, I'll be honest. I had mixed feelings that morning. I was very glad that Paul was participating, and I knew that the preschool experience would be good for him. But there was a little twisting ache in me that felt the loss. My little boy could get along without me! I knew that the relationship between Paul and me would never be quite the same as before. What I didn't know then was that, in that letting go—and in all the others that were to follow—lay all the promise and hope of a truly authentic relationship.

As the children grew older, I sometimes made the mistake of stepping in to try to "make everything okay again," instead of letting them take the consequences of their own choices. For example, I called Paul's teacher once to explain why he hadn't finished his homework, instead of making him responsible for his own explaining. Another time, when a friend of Karen's hurt her feelings, I talked to the girl's mother, instead of leaving it up to my daughter to work out her relationship problems. Eventually, I saw that this robbed them of their chance to learn how to handle their own problems, to take responsibility for their own actions.

Of course, the time came when I could no longer make everything right. I learned in family counseling that no one (not even a loving mother) can be responsible for someone else's *feelings.* I had to learn to let my kids bear their own pain and work out their own solutions to the difficulties of life. It was a hard lesson—for me and for them—and we're still working on it, but we have begun to set each other free. And we're learning that there's a two-way bonus: *in freeing others, we also free ourselves.* It can work the other way, too: *in freeing ourselves, we also free our loved ones.* All of this is true, not only for parents and children, but also for friends, spouses, brothers and sisters—anyone with whom we want an authentic relationship.

Trying to Control

Recently, as I stood in a circle of Christian friends with joined hands, singing "Blest Be the Tie That Binds," I sensed that joyous oneness that belongs to members of the family of Christ. When Christ is the tie, the bonding is truly blessed. But ties that bind are not always blessed. Sometimes they chafe and choke. *Bond* is a two-way word. It can refer either to a very negative thing (captivity, slavery) or to a very positive thing (a uniting force, a tie, a link).

Look at how the word *bond* is used in the Bible. In Ephesians 4:3, Paul says that we are called "to keep the unity of the Spirit in the bond of peace." And in Colossians 3:14, we learn that *love* is "the bond of perfectness." Clearly, bonding in love with another human being is the mountaintop experience of human relationships, and it comes from being unified in the Spirit. That, of course, is very different from *bondage,* which causes bitterness, as it did in the Israelites who were in bondage in Egypt. "And the Egyptians made the children of Israel to serve with rigour: And they made their lives bitter with hard bondage" (Exodus 1:14).

In our part of the world at least, we've grown beyond the institution of slavery—the owning of one human being by another. And yet it is present in subtler forms, such as possessiveness, manipulation, and trying to control. A person who demands the exclusive attention of another almost always loses it. But when we allow our loved ones freedom (within the parameters of our commitment to one another, of course), our relationship can grow and expand in un-dreamed-of ways. I like the image that Henry Nouwen uses of two hands brought together, "not as interlocking fingers but as parallel hands which allow both closeness and separateness."[4] Yes. As *praying* hands!

How can we avoid putting others in bondage to us or allowing ourselves to become bound? Once we've established true intimacy with God and with ourselves, it's much easier to be freeing in our relationships with other people. Yet even then, most of us have some possessiveness, some jealousy, some vulnerable places that stir our defensiveness. Many of these are carryovers from childhood. Somehow, those old hurts reach out like pickaxes, to hook us into *reacting* (acting in an automatic way) instead of *responding* (from the Latin word meaning *to pledge again*). So what are we to do? First, we need to claim God's gift of bonding with others by creating intimate relationships. Having a network of close relationships will give us the security for the second step, which is to confront the problems that arise.

Creating Intimate Relationships

Because intimate friendships are so important, it's worth investing time and energy in creating them. There are a number of specific things we can do that will help foster such close friendships.

Spend Time Together

The first thing necessary is to make it a point to spend time together. That sounds so obvious; and yet you and I know how often we say to casual acquaintances, "Let's get together sometime," and how infrequently we do it! If we really want to develop a close relationship, there is no adequate substitute for time spent in one another's company.

Earlier, I mentioned that my friend Jan and I *scheduled* time together during the budding stages of our friendship. Doing that is a strong message to the other person, as well as to yourself, that this friendship is truly important and that you honestly want to grow in intimacy. It's also a way to learn whether or not the two of you have enough in common to devote time and energy to the relationship. Obviously, we can't be close to everybody, and it's good to find that out early.

I'd suggest scheduling time together on a trial basis for a specific period of time (perhaps six weeks if you meet only once a week; maybe only two weeks if you meet every day). Agree that at the end of that period, you'll each have a choice about whether you want to continue scheduling time together, or want to go back to just seeing each other as the occasion arises. Or maybe you'll want to change the frequency or length of your meetings. Jan and I have gone from daily scheduled meetings to weekly ones, but our lives and activities have become intertwined enough that we see or talk with each other almost every day, anyway. Still, I know that it was that early *planning* of time together that got our friendship off the ground.

Get Past Small Talk

Henry Brooks Adams wrote that "one friend in a lifetime is much; two are many; three are hardly possible." I think there's some truth in that, because most of us connect with one another in a superficial way only. We talk about our work, our families, our health, or the weather, but seldom do we discuss things that really touch deep places in us. By being genuinely interested in the other person, though, we can learn to steer our conversations away from small talk into things that have real significance for us. That's *necessary* for growing closer.

For example, when there's a pause in the conversation, we might open up a real sharing of self by saying something like the following:

"I'd like to get to know you better. Would you tell me what a typical day is like for you?"

If you're in someone's home for the first time, you might ask, "Which one of your possessions means the most to you?" (This leads to marvelous discussions about *why* it's so precious to your friend. Usually, the reason is far beyond the object itself.)

Or, after you have developed enough trust to feel safe with each other, you might reach a little deeper: "I'd like to know something about your childhood. What were your parents like?"

Or, "Everybody has dreams. If you could have everything the way you wanted it, what would your life be like?"

You might share with your friend some problem of yours and then give her/him an opening by asking, "What's the biggest challenge in your life right now?"

Or offer them a chance to share the lessons life has taught them by asking such things as: "What helps you the most when you're worried about something?" or, "What gives you the biggest lift when you're tired or feeling down?" or, "What person would you say has had the greatest influence on your spiritual life?" This might lead to a discussion of books, or memories of teachers or other mentors, and it can also be a wonderful door-opener into a deep sharing of faith between the two of you, a real gift from God, a *grace* beyond measure.

Don't Force Intimacy

There is, however, a vital caution that needs to go along with the above-mentioned attempts to move from small talk to deeper matters. It is this: closeness cannot be forced. To try to do so is an intrusion on the other's privacy. We don't want people to feel as if we're reporters trying to "capture" them in our notebooks. Ask questions sparingly, and only if it's clear that the other person *wants* to share. It's one thing to express sincere interest with an occasional question, but quite another to invade someone's personhood by asking probing questions about matters that are none of our concern.

A friend recently told me about a woman who tried to develop a friendship with her. "Sue" came on so strong—with frequent phone calls, unannounced visits, personal questions about private things, and repeated demands for attention—that my friend began to feel gobbled up. "It was as if Sue wanted to take over my life, and I didn't know how to stop it," said my friend. "So eventually, I just withdrew."

Aim for Balance

A related problem develops when one person monopolizes the relationship. True friendships involve mutual sharing, so be aware of *balance.* Don't do all the asking or all the talking! In an article for *Guideposts,*[5] Marilyn Norquist told about her experience as manager of a half-way house for former psychiatric patients. One lady in her care was a continual complainer. Every time Marilyn gave her any attention, the patient went on and on and on about her problems. After consulting with the supervising psychiatrist, Marilyn decided to confront the patient.

" 'Eleanor, I'm becoming more and more angry with you and you should know it. You whine at me unendingly about your troubles. . . . You refuse my friendship except in terms of your own illness. I'm tired of it. . . . If you want to be my friend, you'll have to become interested in something outside of yourself.' "

Several days later, Eleanor asked Marilyn to play Parcheesi with her, and as the game progressed, the patient began to whine and complain. "Eleanor. Be still!" said Marilyn.

"There was an uncomfortable silence. Finally Eleanor spoke. 'Marilyn, what did you do yesterday?' "

"I stared at her," Marilyn Norquist remembers, "blinking with the newness of it. For the first time since I had known her, she had reached outside her[self] . . . to the world around her. . . . The following weeks demonstrated that her simple question had been a breakthrough. Eleanor had glimpsed the meaning of mutuality."

It was as if a mirror had been thrust in front of the patient. After that, she did make it a point to ask about other people's lives and concerns, and she gradually began to form relationships. Perhaps we all need to look into that sort of symbolic mirror now and then, to see whether or not we are dumping our garbage on someone without helping to lift *their* load.

Process Junk

Probably the most valuable key to maintaining intimate relationships is to talk about our issues as they come up. Some friends of mine decided, when they were first married, to have a rap session every Friday night and tell each other anything that was bothering them about their relationship. It was a good thing to do and it kept them close. So why did they gradually let go of the practice?

"I don't know," said my friend, "but I do know that over the years, we often swallowed our negative feelings. When something bothered me, I was likely to say to myself, 'Oh well, I can put up with that.' I didn't want conflict and neither did Joe. Of course, the trouble is that each of those unfaced issues became a brick of resentment, and bricks build walls. We are working now to break down those walls, but it would have been so much easier to deal with them brick by brick, as they came up."

That's just as important in a close friendship. My friend Jan and I decided, from the very beginning, that we'd process our junk as it comes up. For example, as we were standing around after church one day, she said to her husband, "Marilyn reminds me so much of Rebecca" (a woman from their former hometown, name changed). It wasn't until several weeks later that Jan mentioned a lady in her former hometown who was a self-righteous martyr. In the course of the conversation, she called her by name. You guessed it—Rebecca. I went home that day feeling very hurt and, well, yes, a little angry. Did Jan really think I was like that? If I had just swallowed my feelings, there would have been an invisible wedge in our newly discovered closeness. But the next day, I brought it up, and Jan told me that Rebecca and I simply *looked* a little alike. Then she reassured me that I was not at all like Rebecca in any other way. How glad we both were that we got that cleared up.

Because Jan and I talk a lot about our feelings, the relationships in our lives, and many other personal things, we often find that, after we've had lunch together, there's something that feels unfinished or uncomfortable. When that happens, we call each other and say, "I've got to process a twinge." Sometimes it's just a little thing we wish we hadn't said, or something that didn't come out the way we meant it, or something the other person said that stung a little. I think it's this practice of "processing our twinges" that makes it possible for us to be completely open with each other when we're together, not having to weigh our words or hide behind defenses.

If I could give one piece of advice to those who want intimate relationships, it would be this: process your junk as it comes up. It's the sort of thing that helps people to stay close in any relationship. Jesus knew this when he said, "First be reconciled to thy brother, and then come and offer thy gift" (Matthew 5:24).

Share Honestly from the Heart

Part of becoming intimate is coming to know each other's deepest truths. Sometimes this means sharing our pain, being vulnerable. This isn't an easy thing to do. Probably all of us have felt betrayed at some time in our lives when we've told another about our pain. Perhaps the person we told it to passed it on to others, gave us unwanted advice, or even rejected us because of it. That's why it's important to find out who our safe people are. Charles L. Whitfield, in his book, *Healing the Child Within,* suggests a share/check/share method of discovering this.[6]

> We can share just a bit of our feelings with selected people. Then we check their response. If they don't seem to listen or if they try to judge us or if they immediately try to give us advice, we may not wish to share any more feelings with them. If they try to invali-

date our feelings, or if they reject us and certainly if they betray us by talking about us and especially our confidences then they are probably not "safe" to continue sharing with.

Why does Whitfield suggest listening without giving advice? Except when they specifically *ask* for your opinion or advice, most people really *don't want that.* All they actually want is to be truly heard. I've found that when someone gives me unasked-for advice, it often puts me in an emotional bind. If I don't do what they've suggested, I begin to feel uncomfortable around them. I'm especially reluctant to talk with them anymore about the situation in question, because it puts me on the defensive. I feel that I need to explain why I didn't do what they suggested. However, there *are* times when I really do want a friend's opinion about something, and then I ask for it. Good friends understand the difference.

When your friend is hurting, it may be necessary for him/her to tell and retell her story. Tears may be shed each time. Don't be too quick to label this self-pity. It's a grieving process that must be gone through on the way to healing. If you can just be there for your friend, listening to her feelings, letting her know you care, the pain will become a little bit less each time the story is told, until finally she is able to let go. Friendship offers no greater privilege than to be the one who listens to the story that heals.

Learn to Listen

How many times have you needed to talk to someone about a problem or concern, brought the subject up, and then felt that the other person couldn't care less? Let's face it. We *are* more concerned about our own problems than anyone else's. That's human nature. Most of us would also rather hear ourselves talk than to listen to someone else. However, there is a wonderful *adventure* awaiting us if we can learn to truly listen.

Perhaps the most necessary requisite for being a good listener is rather hard to do at first. We need to set aside whatever is going on in our own mind and truly pay attention to the other person. One thing that makes this possible between close friends is the fact that the listener knows that he or she will eventually have a turn to talk and be truly heard. Sometimes physical things, such as leaning toward them and looking into their eyes, will help us to keep our focus on them. Often, our thoughts start racing ahead to think of what *we* might say next. This is because we think we need to impress the other person. If we notice this happening, we need to remind ourselves that truly listening to another is a far more valued gift than the most profound statement we might make. It's true!

It's also important not to "steal the conversation." This happens when we say, "Oh yes, that happened to me once," and then take over with the telling of our own story. On the other hand, it's good to give little indications that we're truly hearing what the other is saying. These may be just nods of the head, or short comments such as, "I see," or, "Really?" or, "I know how that feels." It's just essential to let our friend finish his or her story, and to get it all out. There is such healing in that. And it so rarely happens.

Here's a recent example from my own life. While Jan was out of town for a couple of days, some things came up that were quite heavy emotionally for me. When Jan called to say she was home, I asked about her trip and listened until she finished telling about it. Then she asked how things had been with me. I told her about my problem and she said, "Tell me all the feelings that went with that." I had a hard time talking because I kept crying, but Jan simply waited and listened. Once it was all out, I breathed a deep sigh.

In the days that followed, we talked about it a couple more times, and then I completely let go of it. All of the energy I had bound up in it was dissolved, gone. Now, as I look back on that time, I can hardly imagine how it felt, the pain is so completely healed. Truly, a listening friend is a healer of the highest order.

Pray Together

Because I believe that the deepest, truest intimacy is anchored in the love of God, there is no better way to grow in friendship than to pray together. The little intercessory prayer group that meets on Thursday afternoons at our

church is one of the most precious things in my life. No
overwhelming miracles have emerged from those small gatherings, although we have seen the Spirit at work in many
ways. But beyond that, we have laughed together, cried together, and ministered to one another in ways that touch the
hem of Christ's garment. And when we close by joining
hands and praying the Lord's Prayer, we are like those little
drops of mercury Karen and Mrs. Moore played with—
suddenly bonded into oneness.

With other friends, prayer may take the form of just being
silent together in the presence of God. This, too, can be a
blessed knitter of souls that bonds without bondage.

The Candlelighting Prayer

The second part of claiming God's gift of bonding without
bondage is to be honest about the problems in our relationships and begin to deal with them with Christ's help. Such
problems often stem from childhood traumas or other unresolved griefs that keep hooking us back in to negative
attitudes, even though the original problem is long past. One
of the most precious gifts our Lord has given me is a way of
prayer that helps to release those old hooks. I call it the
Candlelighting Prayer.

In our church, we have a silent watch from 8:30 P.M. on
Maundy Thursday until 8:30 A.M. on Good Friday. People
sign up to spend one hour at the church during the night, to
watch with Christ, as He asked His disciples to do that night
in the Garden of Gethsemane (Matthew 26:40). Several years
ago, as I was sitting in the semidarkness of the sanctuary in
the middle of the night, I closed my eyes, and it seemed to
me that Jesus stood at the altar, his robes streaming with
light, His arms raised in blessing. And He led me into a
prayer that has helped to heal many broken places in my
relationships. I've taught it to hundreds of others at retreats,
and through it, by the grace of the Holy Spirit, Christ has
brought about some marvelously healing changes in relationships. I'd like to pass it on to you.

Try to find a time when you can be alone for about fifteen
minutes. First, read through this section on the candlelighting prayer. Or you may wish to tape-record it so you can

follow the prayer without having to refer to the book. Stretch a little and take a few deep breaths. This will help you to relax so it'll be easier to sit restfully. Then close your eyes and (this step is essential) *ask the Holy Spirit to guide your prayer.*

Begin by going, in your mind's eye, to a church that you love. It is night time, the church is empty, and a soft whisper of reverence comes over you when you go in and close the door, shutting out the busy world so you can be alone in the stillness with God. Let the filled silence fall on your heart. Soak warm peace into your soul.

Now notice that in the back pew to your left is an unlighted candle. Pick up that candle and begin to walk down the aisle toward the front of the church. As you do, you'll see Jesus standing there, in front of the altar. He is the risen, transfigured Christ. His robes are of flowing light, and His arms are raised in blessing. There is a warm, compassionate smile on His face. Walk slowly toward Him now, in the semidarkness. As you do, you will notice that a light brighter than many candles is shining out from the center of our Lord's chest.

When you are close enough, raise your unlighted candle to His light. As you do this, there will be a sudden burst of radiance as your candle flames up, receiving His light, which is the light of pure love, *the light that bonds without bondage.* Let that happen now. This is a light that warms but never burns, so allow it to extend downward from the tip of your candle, through your arm, and into your own heart. Feel the light of Christ's love permeating your entire being—body, soul, and spirit.

Bow to Jesus now, and turn around. You will notice that the church is no longer empty. In the pew to your right, near the front of the church, sits your mother. It doesn't matter whether or not she is still alive on the earth. She lives forever within you. Walk up to your mother and greet her in your usual way. Now notice that there is something in her hand. It is an unlighted candle. Become aware again of the light emanating from your heart. See it traveling down your arm, through your candle, lighting your mother's candle. See it moving from her candle into her heart, and notice that, by

His light, the two of you are *bonded together in love.* Now say to your mother, "We are one in the love and light of Christ."

Now notice that across the aisle to your left another person sits, holding an unused candle. It is your father. Greet him in your usual way. Become aware again of that glow of Christ-love shining forth from your heart, and allow it to travel down your arm, through your candle, lighting your father's candle and extending into his heart. Say to your father, "We are one in the love and light of Christ."

Now notice who is sitting in the next pew. It might be your brother or sister, your spouse, or your children. Light the candles of your family members, one at a time, staying with them until the light of Christ arcs across between you, bonding you in His love. Then continue walking down the aisle, stopping at each pew until you see who is sitting there. (It may be a person from your past, a friend, someone you love or someone you find it hard to love.) Let the Holy Spirit lead.

Sooner or later, you will come to someone toward whom you have some negative feelings. Notice that even this person is holding up to you an unused candle. Even though it may be difficult, walk up to that person who is hard to love, and touch the tip of your candle to theirs. As you do so, let the light that shines forth from your heart—Christ's light—go out through your candle, igniting the wick of that person's candle. Watch as the light travels through their arm, into their heart. Now say to that person, "We are one in the love and light of Christ."

When you have walked all the way to the back of the church, lighting the candles of all you pass on the way, turn around, bow again to Jesus, and allow your consciousness to return to the present, still holding the light of Christ within your heart.

If you allow yourself to fully experience this prayer, there may be some tears as old walls are penetrated by love. That's all right. In fact, such tears can be a real gift. They are like the tears that are shed at a joyous homecoming.

The reason that this prayer is effective is that, by the grace of the Holy Spirit, changes are caused in your spirit, which is the starting point of all lasting change for the better. Of course, the warm feelings that are a gift of this prayer may be replaced by old and new annoyances, but as you continue to pray this way for those you love, the changes will gradually become more lasting. You may notice that you are not running all of the old hurts through your mind as much as you used to do. You may find it easier to let those you love live true to their own leadings. You may begin to see the light of Christ shining from the face of the taxi driver, the store clerk, a casual acquaintance.

Here are two things you can do to keep the bondage out of your bonding: (1) Pray the candlelighting prayer every morning for those you will be with during the day, especially focusing on those with whom you have close relationships; and (2) whenever those pickaxes of jealousy, possessiveness, or the need to control threaten to put an intimate relationship in bondage, take a two-minute break. (You can always excuse yourself for that long.) Close your eyes and return to that church. Meet Jesus there, receive His light, and light the candle of your intimate other, allowing yourself to fully experience the bonding (unity of spirit) that is God's gift to you. Then carry it with you in your heart. I think you'll be surprised at the freeing effect this will have on your relationships. It might not be instantly noticeable, but *as the bondages are gradually released, the bonding will surely increase!*

So we claim God's gift of *connecting* with others, by first developing greater intimacy with Him and with ourselves, and then by working at creating intimate friendships. When we feel safe enough to let go of the tightrope, we'll know first-hand that there *is* a spiritual net there—a net that will make it possible for us to rise again and soar together, like birds who fly in formation while preserving their individuality.

NOTES

1. Lesley and Earl Barfoot, "Intimacy," in *Alive Now!* (September/October, 1983), pp. 4–5.

2. Jerry Greenwald, *Creative Intimacy* (New York: Pyramid Books, 1975), p. 42.

3. Rose Franken, *Claudia* (New York: Samuel French, 1941).

4. Henry Nouwen, "Can You Be Intimate with More Than One Person?" in *U.S. Catholic* (July, 1979), p. 8.

5. Marilyn J. Norquist, "To Love the Unlovable," *Guideposts* (May, 1971), pp. 22–24.

6. Charles L. Whitfield, *Healing the Child Within* (Pompano Beach, Fla.: Health Communications, 1987), p. 82.

CHAPTER 6

The Gift
of Expanding Ideas

Wisdom is the principal thing; therefore get wisdom: and with all thy getting get understanding. Exalt her, and she shall promote thee: she shall bring thee to honour, when thou dost embrace her. She shall give to thine head an ornament of grace: a crown of glory shall she deliver to thee.

Proverbs 4:7–9

Except for a hurried trip to the grocery store, I've been cooped up in my basement office for several days, trying to meet a deadline. But tonight after dinner, I decided to reward myself by taking a walk. It's been a glorious fall day, with just enough crispness in the air to make my old wool parka feel exactly right. The greens of trees and grass are just beginning to give way to yellows, reds, and golden browns. I walked straight west until the sidewalk ran out and my feet connected with the earth. Mmm. Good.

For quite a while, I looked downward as I walked, absorbing the changing of seasons in the weeds, prairie grass, and rich Nebraska soil under my feet. Then, in a shift of perspective, I looked up at the sky, and it almost knocked me breathless. In all the fifty-seven years of my life, I've never seen a sky quite the color of tonight's. It was a brilliant *turquoise,* painted with flaming pink clouds that simply made me gasp.

Suddenly, right out there in that field, some tightly wound

part of me broke free, expanding outward into all of that beauty. It was as if I, too, were sky and clouds. A shiver of joy shot through me. I watched until the pink was almost gone, and then I turned and headed home, feeling liberated, released, free to be more than I have ever been before. Now, as I sit here in my room, I am still partly sky and cloud, partly browning grass and turning leaves. For the moment at least, I am more than myself.

I have the same kind of awareness when I read or hear or touch a shining new idea that breaks through some of my old, limiting, cramping thoughts. Something inside of me is suddenly liberated, and I know that I'll never be imprisoned in the old way again. It's a grace that can never be earned, a gift that is already given, waiting only for my readiness to claim it. At such times I realize there's a whole wide sky of expanding ideas and fresher, deeper meanings awaiting me!

Letting Our God Grow

One area where I need to open up to new meanings is my idea of God. When I was a child, I sometimes envisioned God as a hostile, punishing parent. At other times I thought of Him as a Santa Claus who would grant my wishes if I'd just be a good girl. I think that's pretty normal for children. But I'm becoming aware that, even as an adult, I sometimes slip back into such limiting views of God. I also find that the God I say I believe in and the one my actions show I believe in are sometimes at odds.

Recently I told a group of friends that things seemed to be running quite smoothly in my life, after several months of stress. As soon as the words were out of my mouth, an old childhood superstition followed it: "I guess I'd better knock on wood." Now, I say I believe in a loving God who wants only the best for His children, and I don't think of myself as superstitious. Yet here I was, hesitating to say things were going well for me because of an unconscious fear that God might hear and decide it was time for the bad stuff to start again! Isn't that silly?

It is limiting views about God (usually unconscious) like this that I need to become more and more aware of. Once I recognize them, I can consciously move beyond them. Sometimes, just *noticing* such contradictions helps me to let go of them.

Another way my beliefs and my actions don't match shows up when I have a problem. I offer it to God, ask for His guidance and help, and tell Him that I trust Him to bring about a good solution. But ten minutes later, I take it all back, forcing *my* will on the situation. This happened a while back when a friend and I had a misunderstanding and both of us went away angry. I prayed about it and asked for God's guidance in resolving the problem. Then I spent some time in silent listening but it seemed that no answer came. I tried to wait for some guidance but my emotions kept jabbing at me, so I called my friend and tried to straighten things out. It was the wrong thing to do. We both needed a cooling-off period. I realized then that I should have waited until I sensed God's leading before I called. Though she and I did eventually get our misunderstanding straightened out, *God's* timing would have been best. The lesson I needed to learn was this: when I say I trust God, I need to show it by my actions.

My idea of God and my knowledge of Him need to expand so that He may become truly the God of my whole life. I want to let Him be God of my mind and heart, of my body, soul, and spirit; God of all my relationships; God of my work, of my waking and sleeping, walking and learning; God of the thoughts I think, the words I say, and the actions I take or refrain from taking. And yes, I especially need Him to be the God in my suffering, in my drudgery, in my physical and emotional pain. And to be able to *receive* Him into all of the huge rooms and little corners of my life, I have to stop limiting the way I think of Him.

Here are some ideas that I have found to be mind- and spirit-stretchers.

What if we were to open up all the doors and windows of our minds? Surely we'd find that God is not limited to one denomination, that no creed could possibly contain a description of all that God is. Would we also be able to see that God is not confined to any time or place? That He is not only the God of our earth but also of the sun and moon and stars, and beyond that, all the galaxies, and the whole universe . . . and universes as yet unknown to us? And that He is God of all that is beyond that, and beyond that, and beyond that? And if the physical reach of God in the universe is impossible for us to comprehend, what about the dimensions within the atom that are spaceless, timeless—the possibility of realities within realities within realities, and levels of being beyond anything our human minds can now conceive? To meditate on all of this helps me see how much I've limited God in my mind, and causes me to cry out in wonder, as the Psalmist did, "What is man that thou art mindful of him, and the son of man that thou dost care for him?" (Psalm 8:4).

Another idea that is very exciting to me is the concept of the *hologram,* which is a three-dimensional likeness projected into space by a laser beam. Recently I visited the Museum of Holography in New York City. There I saw a drinking glass sitting on a shelf, but when I reached out to touch it, I found that only the bottom half was real. The top half was projected from a holographic plate by a laser beam. I could hardly believe what I was seeing and touching. Such a mix of physical and projected reality called for a rethinking of my concepts about what is real. The fascinating thing is that, *if the holographic plate is broken, any piece of it when struck by a laser beam will reconstruct the entire image!* In other words, the whole image is present in the least little part of it!

When I think about holography, it becomes a concept that expands my horizons. Not very long ago, the idea of the whole being all there in a part of the whole was unthinkable. Researchers had to suspend their old ideas about the nature of reality in order to discover this exciting fact. Yet the laws and principles on which holography is based have always existed. There is a parallel in the spiritual world. Certainly all of God's truth is available to us and has been since the world began, but He is able to reveal it to us only to the extent that we are ready and open to receive it.

The truth of the hologram adds depth and breadth and height to my appreciation of Jesus' words, "The kingdom of God is within you" (Luke 17:21). Is it possible that you and I then could project a true picture of the kingdom of God? The possibility is always there, but we are only broken pieces, in need of the laser beam of God's love. Perhaps, the more we allow His light to shine in us and through us, the more truly we will project the image of the One who created us. It's exciting to think about!

So many thrilling discoveries are being made in physics today, and more and more hard-nosed, proof-demanding physicists are affirming that there is a reality that is beyond the physical. Scientists are beginning to find concrete evidence of what believers have always known: that physical reality grows out of spiritual reality. "And God said, Let there be. . . ." Creation is an eternal process. To me, that's very exciting.

We Christians make a big mistake if we try to separate ourselves from the world of science. Jesus said, "Ye shall know the truth, and the truth shall make you free" (John 8:32). Why should we shy away from investigation into the mysteries of God's world? Emerson said, "All that I have seen teaches me to trust the Creator for all that I have not seen." Since all truth is God's, we don't have to be afraid of truth in any aspect of life, even though new light on any aspect of thought or theory can turn our previous human thinking upside down. This can be scary. Imagine how people felt when they learned that the earth was not the center of the universe, or even of the solar system. That's why we need to constantly remember that God is always bigger and beyond any scientific theory. Always there will be the unknown, the wonderful mystery, but God created us with a hunger and thirst for truth. Let us use it wisely and prayerfully, to receive the gift of expanding ideas!

Of course, the question arises: how do we know which new ideas about God are valid? It's a very important question. The best indicator is whether or not the new concept fits with what we know about God from Scripture. By that I don't mean a verse extracted out of context, but the overall sensing of who God is that comes from spending time with Him in the pages of the Bible. I want to keep making room for new truths, keep asking unanswerable questions. Yet, as my ideas about God and His vastness grow, I also need to keep checking them out against what I know to be true of Him from Scripture.

Building an Inner Library

But can we really keep learning new things about God from Scriptures that have been read and studied and theologized about for nearly two thousand years? How can there be anything yet undiscovered there? Yet there is. The truth contained in the Bible is inexhaustible. God can use *any* passage to speak in new and overturning ways today, to you, to me, if we're open to His living Voice there.

That means that even our views about the Bible need to grow with our maturity in faith. I have a lovely friend in her eighties who has a marvelous knowledge of the Bible. She has acquired it over many years, through daily Bible reading. But Anna has a wisdom and a knowledge that is more than just being able to quote verses. (In fact, she rarely does that.) The wisdom of all the characters who people the pages of Scripture has become hers. Anna has *within her* the lessons that God's people learned—from their mistakes, from their right and wrong decisions, from their circumstances in life, from their relationships with God. The parables of Jesus come readily to Anna's mind at appropriate moments.

All of her biblical knowledge is like an inner library for my friend, and she often draws on it. It has caused me to want to build my inner library, too, so I'm trying to be more faithful to daily Bible reading, knowing that whatever I put into my mind from God's word will guide me and lead me, even when I'm not consciously aware of it. This is a wonderful secret of wisdom, a *grace* beyond all imagination.

By Letting Go of Rigidity

At the same time, we need to open our minds and hearts to receive that grace in fresh ways. To claim the gift of expanding ideas and to learn more from Scripture it's essential to let go of rigidity in interpreting Bible passages. I need to free myself from looking at Scripture from just one angle, so that familiar incidents, stories, and parables may come to life for me in new ways. I need to allow the Word of God to speak to me on many different levels. The place to begin, of course, is with the *historical,* factual level, but we needn't stop there. Often, there is also a *symbolic* meaning behind the words. And then there must be a *personal* application of the same truth.

Look, for example, at the story of the blind beggar as recorded in John 9:1–41. Jesus really did give sight to this man who was born blind. It actually happened. But the story can also become a symbol of the truth that Jesus is able to give us spiritual sight.

Let's see how a symbolic understanding of this story might help our ideas expand. Jesus anointed the eyes of the blind man with clay and then told him to go wash it off. The man came back, seeing. Symbolically, this shows me that gaining spiritual sight requires two-way action between Christ and me. Our Lord is the miracle worker, but I must also do my part, by washing away the mud that has become encrusted over my spiritual eyes. Could that mud be all of my rigid views that limit my ability see with fresh eyes?

After we've looked at the historical and symbolic levels of a Bible story, there is still at least one more level—practical application to our personal lives. In this case, I need to ask myself, "In what ways am I spiritually blind?" Could it be that I spend too much time working on my own spiritual growth and not enough reaching out to others in the name of Christ? Once I've become aware of my spiritual blind spots, I can ask Jesus to heal them. But, as the Pharisees in this story discovered, He can't heal me if I don't know I'm blind.

The more we open ourselves to Scripture on many levels, the more it has to say to us.

By Using the Imagination

Another way to gain fresh insights into Bible incidents is to use our imaginations. I do this by entering into a scene in my mind, and trying to view the event through the eyes of one of the people involved.

Take, for example, the wedding in Cana (John 2:1–11). When, in my imagination, I placed myself in the scene and tried to see Jesus' first miracle through the eyes of His mother, I had to chuckle at the humanness of this mother-son interaction. Mother tries to get her Son to do something; He declines; and she goes ahead and starts making arrangements with the servants for what the Son has said He wasn't going to do. Of course, Jesus does turn the water into wine.

But the thing that dawned on me when I got into that scene was that, though it was His first public demonstration, this wasn't Jesus' first miracle after all! How do I know? I've seen the incident through His mother's eyes! She wouldn't have suggested He do something about the lack of wine, unless she already knew He could. He had probably been performing quiet miracles at home for years. Somehow, that realization gave me a new feeling of intimacy with Jesus and His family. It expanded my concept of who He is.

By Developing My Relationship with Christ

The best way to learn more about God and to receive more from the Bible is to develop an ongoing relationship with Christ through daily companionship with Him. By entering into Scriptural scenes, by spending time alone with Him, focusing all of my attention on Him for at least a few minutes every day, I can begin to sense His character, the truth of His identity, and how He reveals God to us. This will help me weed out any new concepts that are not congruent with who He is.

When I'm feeling lonely, I can close my eyes and be with Jesus in the Garden of Gethsemane; and then I know that He, too, experienced loneliness and is with me in mine. When I'm tried, or tempted, I can mentally go into the desert with Him and be ministered to, as He was, by angels.

Spending time with Him in these Scriptural scenes helps me to *know* Him, to have a personal relationship with Him. And this gives me a true basis for testing new concepts.

Wisdom—The Treasure at the Center

Probably the best gift we can receive is the gift of wisdom.

What is wisdom? How can we define it? Here's a definition I received recently: "Wisdom is putting knowledge to work appropriately."[1] Yes; for what good is knowledge unless it is applied to life in some way? Wisdom, I think, is rather like a rose—something that is never final or static, whose beauty is in its living-ness. Wisdom unfolds itself like a rose of countless petals, and the deepest wisdom always ends in mystery. We cannot explain it. We can only live it.

My friend Anna, whom I mentioned earlier, is such a wise person, she should have a Ph.D. in "Wisdom." Although Anna's formal education stopped many, many years ago, her learning abilities are still zooming down the track like the Colorado Zephyr. She reads voraciously, takes study courses through the mail, attends lectures, works on improving herself, and finds her greatest satisfaction in sitting with a friend listening to taped lectures or discussing books that both have read. But more important than all of that is the fact that Anna has found her center. She knows that she can always go within and tap into God's wisdom. When I ask her advice about a problem, Anna often says, "You already know the answer. It's within you. Let's just sit quietly for a few minutes, to get ourselves centered. Then we'll listen. The Holy Spirit within you knows the solution to your problem. Just listen."

Not always, but very often, an answer comes to me during that time. Or Anna suggests another question for me to ask myself. Rarely does she give direct advice. Sometimes she tells me about a time when she had a similar problem. Most of the time, though, she just keeps turning me back to that *inner connection between the Holy Spirit and my own spirit,* to that place in me that is *accessible to God's grace.*

The exciting thing is that this process has taught me that that inner connection is always there. Always. It's just that sometimes the access to it is blocked. "Behold, I stand at the door and knock" (Revelation 3:20, RSV).

What are some of the blocks that keep our ideas imprisoned in too small a space? And how can we prepare an opening for Christ's unlimited wisdom?

I'd suggest, for one thing, reading the Book of Proverbs, especially chapter 8, or the Book of Wisdom (The Wisdom of Solomon), and soaking your mind and heart in them. Here are just a few verses from Proverbs 8 that may help increase your desire for the gift of expanding ideas. Wisdom is personified here and is speaking:

"Hear; for I will speak of excellent things; and the opening of my lips shall be right things" (verse 6); "Receive my instruction, and not silver; and knowledge rather than choice gold. For wisdom is better than rubies; and all the things that may be desired are not to be compared to it" (vv. 10–11); "I am understanding; I have strength" (v. 14); "Now therefore hearken unto me, O ye children: for blessed are they that keep my ways. Hear instruction, and be wise, and refuse it not" (vv. 32–33); "For whoso findeth me findeth life, and shall obtain favour of the Lord" (v. 35).

Since the Book of Wisdom is part of the Apocrypha, most Protestants haven't read it, but my spiritual director suggested it to me, so I read and meditated on it during one of my twenty-four-hour private retreats. I came away from that time with a precious sense that God really will guide me by His own wisdom, if I ask Him. Here is part of Solomon's prayer for wisdom. I found it meaningful. Maybe you will, too. Throughout, the pronoun *she* refers to Wisdom.

> God of our ancestors, Lord of mercy. . . .
> With you is Wisdom, she who knows your works,
> she who was present when you made the world;
> she understands what is pleasing in your eyes
> and what agrees with your commandments.
> Dispatch her from the holy heavens,
> send her forth from your throne of glory
> to help me and to toil with me
> and teach me what is pleasing to you,
> since she knows and understands everything.
> She will guide me prudently in my undertakings
> and protect me by her glory.
>
> *Wisdom 9:1, 9–12, JB*

From the vantage point of the New Testament, we can see in this description of Wisdom the work of the Holy Spirit who reveals to us the mind of God and guides us into all truth (John 14:26; 16:12–15).

Clearing Out the Back Shelves

In order to be open to God's wisdom, we may need to clear our minds of ideas that are no longer meaningful to us. Sometimes we cling to old, worn-out concepts that are just rattling around in our unconscious minds, causing us to act in ways that are not true to our highest selves. Maybe it's time for a good, old-fashioned spring or fall cleaning of our mental houses—closets, pantry, drawers, and all.

Here's an example of back-shelf thoughts that have held me captive for too long. I'm working on cleaning them out. The problem is one I've mentioned before: I find it very hard to speak up when I disagree with the majority in a group. It's a character trait I'm working on, so I'd like to share some other things I've discovered about how this can be a block to wisdom. Maybe the questions I'm asking myself will help you to examine your blocks, too. For example: What unconscious belief is *behind* my fear that I'll be rejected if I disagree?

In his book, *Do You Hear What You're Thinking?* Jerry A. Schmidt suggests a way to discover and root out those old hindering beliefs.[2] First, stop and listen inwardly to what you're telling yourself about the situation. Here are some of the irrational (normally unconscious) thoughts that I've become aware of that make me hesitant to express disagreement:

If I disagree, my friends won't like me anymore.
Since so many of them think that way, I must be wrong.
It's not nice to disagree.
If it turns out that I'm wrong, they'll shame me.

These thoughts sound silly and childish, precisely because they *are* carryovers from childhood. They may be the result of things people told me as a child, or painful happenings of the past. But as long as I don't recognize them, they'll keep me pinned to old, ineffective ways of handling life. Yet here we are *now*. The past is past. It's a new time in my life. Armed with the fresh-start attitude we talked about in chapter 2, I'm ready to let go of these limiting ideas.

Schmidt suggests asking yourself three questions:[3]

1. Which of these automatic thoughts are true? Which thoughts follow Christian teaching?

2. How do I know whether they are true or false?

3. What are some alternative ways of thinking?

Here are some of the thoughts I had as I worked through the above questions. I honestly can't know *for sure* whether or not my friends will dislike me if I disagree with them. However, I do know that *I* often *gain* respect for people who are not afraid to disagree. Jesus certainly disagreed with the majority of the Jews many times. Did they stop liking Him? Some did, some didn't. Some of my friends may be upset with me if I disagree. I think that most of them will still like me. If they like me because I always agree with them, it's not the real me they like, but their own echo. The fact that their viewpoint is the majority's doesn't necessarily make it right. Most important, if I've prayed about it and my opinion comes from my most honest center, then it is true *for me,* whether or not it is for them.

When I find myself afraid to disagree, I'll try to root out the old negative thoughts by having these positive ones ready to replace them:

> Jesus is my example. He was not afraid to disagree.
> I want my friends to like the *real* me, not a fake.
> I can trust my own inner center. The opinion I express is
>   true for *me,* now.
> True friends don't shame each other.

Of course, the only way I'll know for sure how my friends will react to my opposing opinion is to state it. I'll try to do this in a friendly way. Maybe I'll try it first when the topic is not of great consequence. This will help me build my confidence so that I can be strong enough to stand alone on the more divisive issues, if I truly disagree.

Some of the other false assumptions I've found on my back shelves are:

> I have to be perfect to gain approval.
> Everybody should like me.
> If a family member is upset, it must be my fault.
> I should help everyone who needs it.
> I must never hurt anyone's feelings.
> I should be able to pray all of my problems away.
> The world ought to be fair.

I'm trying to sweep these out because they're really *not* Christian concepts. Besides, they are like tight elastic bands that pinch and cramp, and I want to be open to God's gift of expanding ideas.

Changing Our Inner Script

I am presently working on another outgrown idea. I found myself in a state of anxiety last evening because of uncertainty about future finances. I also felt some anger because of what I perceive to be the unfairness of it. Yet I'm learning that the only person I can change is myself. After I'd prayed about it last night, I became deeply aware of the fact that there is something within me that *knows* exactly what I need and how to move me toward it, even when I'm feeling most insecure. I believe it's the Holy Spirit dwelling within me. What I was led to do first was simply to *feel* my pain and to act it out in harmless ways. I allowed myself a silent scream, tensing every muscle of my body, kicking my feet into the mattress. I pounded my pillow. Then I threw a couple of books down onto the bed as hard as I could. All of this was a physical release that left my body feeling cleared out, relieved. Then I wrote out my feelings in my journal, ending with this prayer: "I have to be healed, Lord. Show me how. Please. Amen." This morning I worked to change my mental script.

Perhaps the procedure I found helpful to me will help you with some aspect of your life that needs healing. Here are the steps I followed today.

Name the area of your life that needs rescripting. For me, today, it was anxiety about finances.

Decide what would make things right for you in that situation. I want to have enough trust in God's caring love and enough confidence in my own self-worth that I won't be fearful about the future.

What would this feel like? It would be a centered feeling, a feeling of being solid, of being held up by strong arms.

Put that into a present-tense, positive statement. "I am centered in God, whole, complete, safe."

After I'd written the above statement, I repeated it several times. At that point, I realized that there was a part of me that didn't believe a word of it! I know from past experience that there is a way to get rid of those limiting concepts. It's by getting them out in the open—bringing the unconscious thoughts into consciousness. So I took a sheet of paper and

separated it into two columns. On the left side, I wrote my
positive statement. Then I was silent for a few moments,
listening for what my false self was saying to contradict it.
I wrote the first objection in the right column. Then I wrote
my statement again, listened inwardly, and wrote the next
objection. I continued in this way until all of the dissenting
statements were out on the page. Here is the way my notebook page looked:

I am centered in God, capable, safe.	I am fragmented, needy.
I am centered in God, capable, safe.	I am hurting, incomplete.
I am centered in God, capable, safe.	I am in inner turmoil.
I am centered in God, capable, safe.	I hurt inside, want to cry.
I am centered in God, capable, safe.	I am afraid of lack.

Now that my fears and negative thoughts were out in the
open, they didn't seem so threatening. As I kept repeating
my positive statement during the day, and reminding myself
of how it would feel to be in that state of mind, it got stronger
and the objecting voice became weaker. By evening, there
was a very encouraging *positive* inner voice, and my notebook page looked like this:

I am centered in God, capable, safe.	I have *been* that way in the past. I can be there again.
I am centered in God, capable, safe.	There *is* a centered place in me that has never wavered. Yes!
I am centered in God, capable, safe.	I can be in that place of certainty now.
I am centered in God, capable, safe.	God's arms hold me up.
I am centered in God, capable, safe.	I am a valuable person.

I am centered in God, capable, safe.

We all have negative thoughts that sometimes tangle up
our life but God has graced us with the ability to transform

our thoughts and thereby better the way we cope with life. Let's claim that gift!

Going on a Metaphor Hunt

In a Bible-based class at our church, I learned a process of expanding one's thinking that is like a rose, opening itself petal by petal, to present new truths.[4] Here's how it works:

1. Think of an incident in which you had very strong feelings. For example, I recently felt left out when a member of my small group asked the other two members of the group for help with a problem she was having, but she didn't ask me.

2. Name (or write down) the feelings and thoughts that are associated with the incident. For example, I overreacted, probably because of some unresolved childhood feelings of rejection, abandonment, self-doubt, and hurt. Some thoughts that went through my mind when I was told about it: Why is she trying to hurt me? Help me to keep from crying, God. I don't want to make a fool of myself. Then, later, turning it in on myself, I heard my childish inner voice say: What's the matter with me that I'm not a good enough friend?

3. Next, find a metaphor or symbol that has something in common with the situation about which you're seeking wisdom. For example, in this case, how about the game of musical chairs? It fits, because someone gets left out each time the music stops.

4. Once you have a metaphor, leave the personal incident behind for a while and just examine the world of the metaphor by asking questions, such as:

a. What is it like in the world of the metaphor? Well, musical chairs can be fun and exciting, but also disappointing and painful. At each round, you risk losing. Of course, there's always the possibility of winning, too. But if you win, you're all alone at the end.

b. What does damage to people? What separates them from each other? The answers may be revealing. For example, needing to win separates. Pushing and shoving and looking out only for oneself does damage to self and others. Taking the game too seriously causes one to be a poor loser.

c. What is there in the world of the metaphor that's

good? In this case, there's the music, the challenge, the fun of the game, the camaraderie.

d. What personal insights are there in this for me? In musical chairs, sometimes one person is left out, sometimes another. Maybe I need to be more aware of the times when *I* leave someone out. Also, that phrase "needing to win" (from question b, above) brings me up short, because I am often competitive. This does separate people. I need to pray about this. Another insight is that, when you're playing musical chairs, you can be playful and spirited, carrying life lightly, or you can be grim and determined so that it all becomes unnecessarily heavy. I realized that perhaps I'd made too much of a big deal out of this real or imagined slight by my friend. I saw that I could choose how I saw the situation. I could feel sorry for myself, or I could focus on the fact that I am usually included, and give thanks for the fact that I *do belong* to a group. Another alternative: talk about it with the group, being honest about my feelings. (This, in fact, I did, and I found out that Cheri didn't mean to hurt my feelings at all. She didn't want to bother me because she knew I had writing deadlines to meet. To extend the metaphor one step further: I'm glad I didn't childishly get mad and quit the game!)

Metaphors are wonderful tools for insight that can expand our thinking in surprising ways.

The Examined Life

Socrates said that "the unexamined life is not worth living." That may be a rather sweeping statement. I do believe, however, that it's possible to stumble all the way through life barely aware of who you are, where you've been, where you're going, or what you're about. Lived that way, life soon becomes meaningless.

Here's an incident that illustrates my point. Recently I was to meet a friend for lunch at a restaurant near the north edge of our town. On the way there, I started thinking about a talk I was going to give the next week. Before long, I found myself looking for a place to park at the *mall,* which is several blocks beyond the restaurant where I was to meet my friend. I could hardly believe I'd done that! Yet I think I often do the spiritual equivalent of that, by just going through my days, caught up in external events and routines, never giving much thought to where I am or where I'm headed.

To try to remedy that, I've been taking just a few minutes at bedtime every night to think back through the events of the day, asking myself these three questions:

1. What did I do wrong, and how can I avoid making the same mistakes tomorrow?

2. What did I do right? (Always, I need to remind myself that it's only because of God's grace that I am able to do *anything* right.)

3. For what am I most thankful?

That last item is *gift* from a time when my youngest son, John, was little. I used to ask him, each night before he went to sleep, "What was the best thing that happened today?"[5] John usually woke up happy and smiling. Maybe it was because he went to sleep with a thankful heart.

If you decide to do this, you may want to close your time of evening reflection with a prayer such as this:

> *Heavenly Father, this day is now over. I offer it back to You, praying that You will expand and magnify the good and erase my mistakes by Your love. This I now claim and affirm, in the name of Jesus Christ.*
>
> Amen.

The Growing Life

When my daughter Karen was in the third grade, she came home from a birthday party with a small plastic bag containing water and (are you ready for this?) one small goldfish. It was her favor from the party. (I've often wondered how the *other* mothers felt about that!) Anyway, we hurried to the store and got a small glass fishbowl and a box of fish food for "Goldie." For Karen, it was the beginning of what I'm sure will be a lifelong love of fish. Before long, she decided that Goldie must surely be lonely; so that was when we acquired "Finny."

After a few weeks, Karen began to feel sorry for Goldie and Finny because they didn't have much room to swim, so she saved her allowance until she had enough to buy a five-gallon aquarium, gravel, a small filter, and a pump. We knew the fish would like their new home, but what we didn't know was that, in only a very short time, they would begin to grow noticeably bigger, even though they had remained the same size all the time they were in the small bowl. Over the years, Karen's ichthyological hobby has grown. She now has several aquariums, from ten to fifty gallons in size. But the fascinating thing about this is the fact that fish grow (or fail to grow) according to the size of their container.

I believe that you and I can grow spiritually to the extent that we're willing to increase the size of our spiritual containers. Trusting the Holy Spirit, Scripture, and our church community to help us filter out anything un-Christian, let's expand the living space of our minds so that we can truly grow spiritually.

NOTES

1. Mary Ruth Howes in a letter to the author, February 6, 1989.

2. Jerry A. Schmidt, *Do You Hear What You're Thinking?* (Wheaton, Ill.: Victor Books, 1983).

3. *Ibid.*

4. This idea, here altered and paraphrased, came from *Education for Ministry,* a course published by University of the South, Sewanee, Tennessee, 1985.

5. I think this idea came from an article or book I read when John was small, but I have no other information about the source.

CHAPTER 7

The Gift of Treasures, Earthly and Heavenly

What else do I have in heaven but you? Since I have you, what else could I want on earth?

Psalm 73:25, 26, TEV

After my father retired, he and my mother took a trip around the world. At each important site they visited, Dad bought Mother a gold charm, unique to that special place. They were all twenty-one-carat gold, many of them quite elaborate, with moving parts. Together, they made up a bracelet that was not only lovely, but one-of-a-kind and irreplaceable. More important still, for Mother it was a cast-in-gold memory. I can still see her sitting there, long after Dad had died, fingering each charm and telling me again about all the loveliness of that time. She'd laugh as she held the Eiffel Tower between her thumb and forefinger and told me of the twenty-six slide photos Dad took of that monument, from every possible angle. And I'd laugh too, remembering childhood vacation trips with Daddy behind the camera. Then she'd spin the blades of the little gold windmill from Holland, and her voice would get soft and her eyes misty as she told about the picnic lunch the two of them had on a grassy knoll near a windmill "just like this one!"

During the last year or so of Mother's life, she started

giving away many of her possessions. Whenever she'd drive to Kearney, she'd bring a car-full of stuff for me to go through. "Keep what you'll use and give away the rest," she'd say. On one of her last visits to our house before her final illness, Mother opened her purse and took out a small brown velvet box. She asked me to sit by her on the couch and close my eyes. Then she fastened her golden charm bracelet on my wrist.

"Oh, no," I protested. "You keep this. It's got all of your last memories of Daddy and of that wonderful trip in it! It's your *treasure.*"

"No, you're wrong about that, dear. The memories are in *here,*" she said, placing her hand over her heart. "And my treasure is not in the gold, but in your father's love."

Mother gave me two gifts that day—a gift of gold, to cherish and enjoy for now . . . and the gift of an unspoken question that could lead me to more lasting wealth: *Where is my real treasure?* The question comes to my mind at the most unexpected times—right in the middle of an argument with my oldest son over money . . . or when I'm about to decide I'm too busy to visit my mother-in-law . . . or when a little needle of envy jabs me because a friend has prettier clothes, or more successful children, or greater talent than I. Again and again that question comes: *Where is your real treasure?* Very often, if I take the time to reflect on the answer to that, it straightens out my perspective. That question is a true grace.

Circulation *vs.* Congestion

The question Mother's comments raised for me calls to mind those beautiful words of Jesus, "Lay not up for yourselves treasures upon earth, where moth and rust doth corrupt, and where thieves break through and steal: But lay up for yourselves treasures in heaven, where neither moth nor rust doth corrupt, and where thieves do not break through nor steal: For where your treasure is, there will your heart be also" (Matthew 6:19–21).

Some people interpret Jesus' words to mean that it's wrong to enjoy earthly things. I don't think that's what He meant at all. The key is in the words "lay up," meaning to amass, to stockpile, to accumulate. I'm convinced that Jesus meant for us to fully use and enjoy all the gifts of His world. Think how He supported His friend Mary's act when she anointed His feet with expensive ointment from an alabaster jar (John 12:3–8). Think about His assertion, "I came that they may have life, and have it abundantly" (John 10:10, RSV). Think about the fact that He was so far from rigid self-denial that He was accused of being a glutton and a drunkard (Luke 7:34). Clearly, our Lord meant for us to enjoy all the treasures of His creation. But we must *keep them moving!*

There is a law of circulation operative in the universe that is true on every level. It is this: a constant rhythmical movement is necessary to maintain health and harmony. It's evident in the patterns of sun and moon, the ocean with its tides, the seasons, the growth of a plant and its return to earth to sprout anew. It's true of every living creature and every cell within each of them.

The opposite of circulation is congestion. Many illnesses are caused by emotional congestion—old pain that has never been released. And think of how many lives are adversely affected by congestion on the freeway.[1]

The law of circulation is basic to all earthly treasures. "Give, and it will be given to you; good measure, pressed down, shaken together, running over, will be put into your lap. For the measure you give will be the measure you get back" (Luke 6:38, RSV). Jesus was not suggesting that we give in order to get. He just wanted us to be aware of the law of circulation, so that our souls would not become sick as a result of congestion. If I clean out my closets a couple of times a year and give away the clothes I no longer wear, I am cooperating with the law of circulation. If I share some of my food with those who don't have enough; if I give away some of my time to a lonely shut-in; if I share my friend with others instead of being jealously exclusive, then I am cooperating with the law of circulation. Like a crowded plant that's replanted in another pot, this *creates space* for growth and enrichment of my own life, in both material and spiritual ways.

I'm sure that Jesus wants me to use and enjoy what I have, even to the point of the overflowing cup. But whatever I am not using and do not need must be kept in circulation. I must not *lay up* earthly treasures. For example, when we built our house, there were six of us living at home. It's a large house with lots of space, and we've thoroughly enjoyed living in it for the past eighteen years. But now that the children are grown, we don't need this big house anymore. We've decided to sell it and find a smaller place. Somewhere there's a family that needs, and will thoroughly appreciate having, this large house.

Of course, that means getting rid of an accumulation of *things*. A house does have a tendency to fill up, doesn't it? So we've been going through things, cleaning our storage room, closets, cupboards, drawers. I've realized that we have so many things we don't need. Congestion! It can creep up on you like a disease. Giving away the extras, the outgrown, the no-longer-needed is giving me a wonderful sense of release. Circulation. It restores life and energy.

The law of circulation is equally in force in money matters. Remember the rich young man who asked Jesus what he must do to be saved and was told to sell all his possessions and give the money to the poor? Jesus didn't have anything against money. But He wants us to rid ourselves of anything that has become more important to us than God. Quite often in the Old Testament, God promises—and then fulfills His promise—material blessings for His people. He blesses Abraham, Isaac, Jacob, and many other chosen ones with material blessings. *But always there is the condition that they put God first in their lives.* "If you are willing and obedient, you shall eat the good of the land" (Isaiah 1:19, RSV). This is a very significant point, not because of the material rewards, but because of the inner change of attitude that is brought about in those who are obedient to God. Greed and acquisitiveness are replaced by compassion. Material blessings can safely be entrusted to those who *truly* put God first, because they recognize that the earthly riches are not for them alone, but are meant for the good of all—the law of circulation again!

This inner spirit of sharing (not laying up) earthly treasures has been borne out by many sincere Christians throughout the centuries. For example, the simple lifestyle of John Wesley, who founded the Methodist Church, is well known. He told his sister, "Money never stays with me. It would burn me if it did. I throw it out of my hands as soon as possible, lest it should find its way within my heart." He often said that, if at his death he had more than ten pounds (about $23) in his possession, people had the privilege of calling him a robber. Near the end of his life he wrote in his journal very simply, "I left no money to anyone in my will, because I had none"[2]

Getting Free of the Bully

In our family, our income fluctuates quite a bit, so there are times when we need every cent of it. There are also, once in a while, times when there is more than we need. Of course we save some for emergencies and for our old age, and put aside something now and then for a trip or special treat. I don't think Jesus would call that laying up earthly treasures. But if amassing money becomes my aim, then it *will* get in the way of my relationship with God.

And I've also noticed an interesting thing. When I hang onto my money for fear there won't be enough, there usually isn't. But if, when things get tight, I can make myself give an extra donation to my church or to another worthwhile cause, the most amazing things happen! Once, when we were in a money bind, I sent an anonymous cash gift to a friend I knew was having trouble financially. It was a very hard decision to part with that money, and as I sealed the envelope, I felt a tightness in my chest that almost made me change my mind, but once I'd mailed it, I immediately felt *unlocked!* The first thing that happened was within me, as I suddenly realized that *I no longer had to be controlled by money.* It couldn't push me around anymore! It was as though I had escaped, once and for all, from a great, huge, hairy ape, who had been shoving and binding and pinching me. It was such a winglike grace of inner freedom that I seemed to be flying. About a week later, I received a completely unexpected payment for reprint rights to something I'd written a year before. It was exactly twice the amount I had given away.

Another example: Last summer, I was scheduled to make a business trip to New York, and I didn't have the right outfit for the meetings I'd be attending. We'd just paid our income tax and some other large bills, so there simply wasn't enough money to buy anything new. As I looked through my closet for something that I could make do, I took out all the things that I was no longer wearing and delivered them to our church's clothing center. Three days later, a friend who had lost weight and then gained it back brought over all of her "thin clothes" and absolutely insisted that I keep them! There were two dresses that were exactly right for New York; but besides that, she gave me several other beautiful dresses, skirts, and blouses, and even an attractive jump suit. Talk about good measure, pressed down, shaken together, and running over!

If you have a need or a lack, maybe you'll decide to try giving something away. It may be just what's needed to relieve the congestion and get the law of circulation back into operation in your life.

The Freedom of Simple Living

I love spending time at our Colorado cabin, and I think it's partly because it gives me a chance to live simply, which in turn helps me to live more deeply. Building a fire in the fireplace to chase away the chill of the early morning some-how puts me in touch with the elements—and with my grandparents who did the same thing—in a way that turning up a thermostat could never do. The bouquet of wild flowers I pick on my afternoon hike up the mountainside graces my table in a way that no florist's arrangement ever could. The drinking water I bring back from the spring has a crisp freshness that makes faucet water taste like liquid plastic. And there's something contemplative about simple living. It's more vertical than horizontal. Its roots sink deep and its branches reach high.

Somehow, accumulating possessions increases the complexity of one's life. I recently talked with a young woman who had gone through a painful divorce after twelve years of marriage to a man who was quite wealthy, but repeatedly unfaithful to her. They had a beautiful home, tastefully deco-rated with expensive furnishings. As they tried to reach a settlement, the couple had terrible arguments over who was going to get which piece of furniture, which paintings, which appliances. Susan told me that she was absolutely devastated each time this happened. She felt a recurring sense of great loss, until one day she had had enough, and she threw up her hands and said, "Just take whatever you want and I'll keep the rest." Then she went into the bedroom and prayed, releasing every possession to God.

As she told me about that day, her face shone. "I have never had such a tremendous sense of relief. I realized that there really was not one thing in that house that I couldn't get along without. It was as if I'd been carrying a backbreaking load of luggage and someone had come along and lifted it off of my back!" Susan is now comfortably settled in a modest home, with simple furniture, a few pieces of art, and a stereo (her one luxury) filling her home with beautiful music. "It's really all I need," she told me, "and you just can't imagine how much *freer* I feel!"

"Hidden Riches of Secret Places"

Susan found that letting go, releasing her possessions to God, *creates a space into which new blessings can be poured.* The heading for this section is from Isaiah, through whom the Lord speaks these words: "I will go before thee, and make the crooked places straight: I will break in pieces the gates of brass, and cut in sunder the bars of iron: And I will give thee the treasures of darkness, and hidden riches of secret places" (Isaiah 45:2–3).

Treasures of darkness . . . hidden riches . . . secret places. What does it all mean? The deep truth of those words is that all the riches you'll ever need are *already yours.* There is imprisoned splendor in every object, every living thing; but especially is this true of you and me. Here is a principle that can change your life: *Every good thing that comes to you from without originated within you, at the place where your spirit connects with God's Spirit.*

This statement does not refer just to material things, although they are not excluded. The material sense of life, however, claims that security is based on possessions, which is simply not true. *Spirit* is the substance, and it appears outwardly as form. Meditate on, and try to see with fresh eyes, those words of Hebrews 11:1 (italics mine): "Now faith is the *substance* of things hoped for, the evidence of things not seen." If you can get that realization planted deeply in your mind and heart, you'll begin to know that your source of richness is within, where your spirit touches God's. It's a whole new way of thinking. Instead of trying to add to your treasures from outside of yourself, you will begin to let the richness that God has to offer pour out from within your own soul, which has centered itself in God. Look anew at Jesus' words, "Seek ye first the kingdom of God, and his righteousness; and all these things shall be added unto you" (Matthew 6:33). Here heavenly treasure (God's presence) and earthly treasure (not always material) mesh.

Over the years, I've done a lot of financial bailing-out of my grown children, but family counseling has helped me to see that this was not really helpful to them because it was keeping them dependent on me, which was not good for their self-esteem. I knew this was true, so I was trying to practice "tough love." My oldest son, Paul, was the hardest to say no to, because he's married and has four little children. Quite a bit of friction developed between Paul (who was used to calling and asking me for money and getting it) and his newly assertive mother. After a particularly difficult phone conversation with my son, in which he'd asked for a very large sum of money and I'd said no, I met with the counselor. She asked, "What is it that you really want to happen in this situation?"

I answered something about being willing to help but not wanting to be taken advantage of. That night, I spent quite a bit of my prayer time just being still before God, "centering down" as some call it; and I got in touch with that place in me where the Holy Spirit dwells. Then I again asked myself the counselor's question. The answer was sure and solid and came from deep within me. "I just want a healing of my relationship with Paul." So that is what I prayed for.

I don't pretend to understand what followed, and it may be hard for you to believe, as it was for me. I did not do *one thing,* except to center myself in God and pray for a healed relationship with my son. Paul called the next day, and I automatically tensed up, expecting another battle, because he usually asks again and again, until I give in. But he did not ask for money! Instead, we had a delightful, friendly, loving conversation, in which we were able to express our deep, unblemished love for each other. After that, I *voluntarily* sent them a modest cash gift, and it was a delight to be able to do that simply because I love my son and his family.

From that day on, Paul's and my relationship has been very clear. It's as if all of the smudges on the window through which we see each other have been washed away. I'm sure there will be other tense moments, as in any relationship, but I truly believe that our relationship has been healed. It is a heavenly/earthly treasure, and I thank God for the wonderful mystery of it. "Seek ye first. . . ."

Centering in God

How do we go about centering ourselves in God? The only answer I know is: by prayer.

God is the only creative principle in the universe, and He withholds nothing from us. But it is only when we put Him first, before and above all things, ahead of all other relationships, before every other desire, that He can pour out His blessings upon us. That's why I've found centering prayer so meaningful. I've written about it elsewhere,[3] so I'll discuss it only briefly here. Because I so often lose my way, I want to tell you about this prayer that has kept bringing me back to putting God first. It's a special way of calling on the name of Jesus. Psalm 9:10 (JB) gives the key to its effectiveness: "Those who acknowledge Your name can rely on You."

About fifteen years ago, at a time when I felt as if my spiritual life had just about dried up, a flyer came in the mail announcing a "Contemplative Prayer Workshop." God certainly knew I needed *something,* and so did I, so I signed up for the weekend retreat. Little did I know what a transforming influence it would have on my life. For the first time ever, I began to know the *indwelling* Christ. It seemed as though

Jesus had been reborn within me. During the days and weeks and months that followed, as I practiced this way of prayer, I began to experience a new wholeness of body, soul, and spirit. It has been the strong, solid undergirding that has kept me from falling off the edge of the earth during times of great pain and stress, such as after my son's serious car accident. It is the handclasp that connects me in a very real way with my Creator.

To try this form of prayer, I'd suggest that you begin with just a few minutes of mild physical exercise. Nothing strenuous. Arm swings, knee bends, stretching and reaching, anything physical that will make it easier to relax during prayer. Then, remembering that the biblical word translated *breath* is the same as the word translated *spirit,* take three long, slow, deep breaths. Sit in a comfortable, straight-up position with your eyes closed, and begin silently to pray:

Lord Jesus Christ, Son of the living God, have mercy on me a sinner.

Some people shorten it to *Lord Jesus Christ, have mercy on me.*

The prayer has simplified itself for me to just a loving calling of His name: "Jesus, Lord Jesus . . . Jesus, Lord Jesus . . . Jesus, Lord Jesus."

Before long, you will notice that your mind has begun to wander. This is perfectly normal and should not be resisted or fought. When I notice that I am thinking of other things, I just say in my heart, "Only You, Lord, only You," and then I return to my prayer . . . "Jesus, Lord Jesus. . . ."

Continue in this prayer for fifteen to twenty minutes. (Setting a timer will free you from having to clock-watch.) When you've finished, open your eyes and give yourself a couple of minutes of transition before getting up to go about your daily routine. You will find that, if you pray the Jesus Prayer regularly, at least once a day (or better yet, morning *and* evening), it will *take up residence within you,* and that your inner mind will be praying it all the time, even when your consciousness is active with external things. I find that the words often rise up from within me during moments of stress, when I take a quick break from my work, as I'm driving or putting in a load of laundry, or pushing a grandchild in a swing. Sometimes I wake up with the prayer in my mind and heart. It's like an early morning greeting from the Beloved One.

The Jesus Prayer is one way truly to practice Paul's advice to "pray without ceasing" (1 Thessalonians 5:17). The prayer, of course, does not bring God closer to you. He is already there. What the prayer does is to open *you* to the inflow of His grace. I've found that each time I say, "Only You, Lord, only You," a layer of earthly dross is blown away by the winds of the Spirit. Gradually I get down to that inner core where my spirit connects with the Holy Spirit. Sometimes I know this has happened and sometimes I don't. Its effectiveness is not dependent on a *feeling*. It just is. And like the Psalmist, I emerge from my prayer time knowing beyond all doubt that "those who know your name can rely on you." It's a whisper of heavenly treasure, precious beyond price.

Laying Up Heavenly Treasure

So we are not to lay up for ourselves treasures on earth, but we are asked to lay up treasures in heaven. How can we do that while we're still living in the world?

Jesus gave us several clues. He said to His disciple John, "Whoever gives you a cup of water to drink because you bear the name of Christ, will by no means lose his reward" (Mark 9:41, RSV). It's wonderful to think that for every kindness that you and I do in the name of Jesus Christ, there is a treasure laid away for us in heaven. Jesus also said that if we are persecuted for His sake, our reward will be great in heaven (Matthew 5:12). Knowing this has been particularly helpful to me, because I have a relative who makes fun of my church and prayer activities. When he calls my prayer group my "kook meetings," I can smile inside, knowing that a deposit has just been made to my heavenly account! Jesus also said that the Father will reward each of us according to our works (Matthew 16:27). (It is true that we are saved by faith, not works, but faith results in works and works result in heavenly treasures.) Even our afflictions can create for us an "eternal weight of glory" (2 Corinthians 4:17).

Being a child of the thirties, I can remember how tough

things got during the Depression. During the recent stock market plunge, however, I became deeply aware that there is a kind of wealth that can't be threatened by any economic catastrophe or market fluctuation. To the extent that you and I invest ourselves in loving and serving others, we'll have a credit balance in the book of heavenly treasures. The dividends will be riches that can never be taken away.

The Ultimate Treasure

What kind of treasure is the treasure in heaven? As I've thought my way through this question, I've come to see that there is no stone wall that separates earthly treasure from heavenly treasure. The long, slender fingers of grace reach into every earthly treasure, if we have the eyes to see. And it works the other way, too. Love, beauty, truth, and all the other intangible graces reach beyond this earthbound life into a heavenly dimension that can never be reduced to microscopic or telescopic study. "For the things which are seen are temporal; but the things which are not seen are eternal" (2 Corinthians 4:18).

The exciting thing is that my spirit is *already* part of that unseen eternal, and so is yours, because we are Christ's! *The real treasure is God Himself in us,* as Paul wrote in 2 Corinthians 4:6–7: "For God, who commanded the light to shine out of darkness, hath shined in our hearts, to give the light of the knowledge of the glory of God in the face of Jesus Christ. But we have this treasure in earthen vessels, that the excellency of the power may be of God, and not of us." Maybe it will help us to understand what this means, if we rethink that breakthrough moment on the mountain when Jesus was transfigured in the presence of Peter and James and John. Some say it was a vision seen in a dream by the three disciples. Those who argue this way point out that Luke says, "Now Peter and those who were with him were heavy with sleep" (Luke 9:32, RSV).

On the other hand, there are those who maintain that a *physical* change took place in the body of our Lord. This argument is supported by the fact that all three disciples saw the same thing at the same time, which just doesn't happen in dreams.

I'd like to offer the possibility of a third alternative. Could it be that there was actually no change in Jesus Himself, but that the change was in the *seeing ability* of Peter and James and John? Could it be that Jesus wore His heavenly body all the time that He walked the earth, even though it was clothed in flesh, but that people couldn't see it because their eyes were not capable of perceiving spiritual reality? And could it be that, for those brief moments on the mountain, Jesus' closest friends actually saw, not with the eyes of the body, but with the eyes of the spirit?

Could it be, too, that right here in my basement office, right there wherever you are, there is another world that is just as real, though unseen and unheard—and that *Christ* is the link between the two? Could it be that, at this very moment, you and I are surrounded by "angels and archangels and all the company of heaven"?

Thinking this way helps me realize that heavenly reality is not far away and inaccessible, but that whispers of it can reach right into my earthly life here and now, if I focus my attention on God. "If thine eye be single, thy whole body shall be full of light" (Matthew 6:22).

I had a wonderfully wise aunt whose life was truly a prayer. When I was a child, Aunt Alta played with me, prayed with me, and best of all, introduced me to her friend Jesus. But little girls grow up and aunts grow old, and one gray December day, I stood by Aunt Alta's bedside at St. Catherine's hospital in McCook, Nebraska, holding her frail white hand. Just before she died, Aunt Alta opened her eyes very wide and said, "There He is! Oh, He is so beautiful!" That memory lingers in my heart, not only because I loved my aunt, but also because, at the time of her death, Aunt Alta was totally blind.

How could I not believe that the spirit has its own eyes, and that every moment of our lives we are truly surrounded and filled with the divine? "Eye hath not seen, nor ear heard, neither have entered into the heart of man, the things which God hath prepared for them that love him. But God hath revealed them unto us by his Spirit" (1 Corinthians 2:9–10).

If we could truly live from our holy center where our spirit touches His, our lives might be transformed and transfigured into peace, glory, and miracle, and all of our earthly treasures would bear the stamp of the heavenly. It's an aim worth pursuing for the rest of our lives.

NOTES

1. Emmet Fox, *Find and Use Your Inner Power* (New York: Harper & Bros., 1937), p. 192.

2. John Wesley, cited by Richard Foster in *Freedom of Simplicity* (San Francisco: Harper & Row, 1981), p. 66.

3. Marilyn Helleberg, *God's Best for You* (New York: Macmillan, 1986), pp. 69–70.

CHAPTER 8

The Gift of the Lightened Load

Take my yoke upon you, and learn of me; for I am meek and lowly in heart; and ye shall find rest unto your souls. For my yoke is easy, and my burden is light.

Matthew 11:29–30

It was only after I'd claimed my luggage at the St. Louis airport that I realized what a big mistake I'd made. My hang-up case was loaded, with two wool suits, a raincoat and a fancy dress, plus a pair of shoes and a purse for each outfit. In the outside zippered pocket was my hairdryer and an extra set of cosmetics, in case my luggage should get lost. (I've had that happen!) I also had a heavy leather briefcase, packed full of files, manila envelopes, books (including a dictionary), and even a lap-top computer. Then there was my suitcase, with a pair of jeans, plenty of lingerie, more cosmetics, a heavy, full-length housecoat, a flashlight, an umbrella, and a sweater (just in case). Oh yes, and a tape recorder, as well as extra tapes and batteries, for recording the interview I'd been sent there to do.

With the hang-up case draped over my back (hangers cutting into the flesh of my left hand), and the briefcase tucked uncomfortably under my right arm, I picked up the suitcase with my right hand and started down the long concourse toward the lobby. I had to stop every few steps and rearrange my load. Just as my back was starting to give out, a young man wearing a clerical collar walked up and offered to help.

"Oh, thank you *so much,*" I said. "What a relief!"

As we walked together, he told me that he was returning home after a week and a half of traveling. When I noticed that he had only one small, soft nylon satchel, I suddenly felt absolutely ridiculous. I was going to be in St. Louis for only two days!

"How in the world do you do it?" I asked.

"One of the most valuable things I learned in seminary is that our Lord wants us to 'travel lightly' through life," said the young man.

"But what does that *mean?*" I asked, realizing that he was talking about something infinitely more important than the luggage we were carrying.

"There is only one thing necessary, one single holy assignment for travelers through life, and if you follow it faithfully, you will be truly free. That one thing is this: let *nothing* become more important to you than Christ. Keep that rule, and all the things you are in bondage to will begin to fall away or be transformed. Then you won't have to find freedom. It will find you."

That night in my hotel room, I couldn't seem to get that young man and his comments out of my mind. I started rummaging through my briefcase and could hardly believe it when I realized that the one thing I'd forgotten to bring was my Bible. Thanks to the Gideons, though, I found one in the bedside drawer and looked up the passage in Luke, in which Jesus sends out the twelve disciples "to preach the kingdom of God and to heal. And he said to them, 'Take nothing for your journey, no staff, nor bag, nor bread, nor money; and do not have two tunics' " (Luke 9:2–3, RSV).

I realized, of course, that I'd burdened myself with a great number of nonessential things on the trip to St. Louis, and I resolved that, after this, I'd gladly trade an impressive wardrobe and extra equipment for freedom of movement and a pain-free back!

But there was a much bigger issue that gnawed at me. Thinking about my talk with the young minister in the airport, I began to see that traveling lightly meant more than just not taking along a bunch of material things (although it meant that, too). One phrase of his seemed to keep twining around my thoughts, as persistently as ivy. It was his comment that "the things you're in bondage to will begin to fall away or be transformed."

I had been thinking a lot about bondage, not only because I'd been dealing with some blockages in my own life, but also because this seems to be a problem for every person. People often tell me about the pains, frustrations, and despairs of their lives, and again and again I note the common denominator is a lack of inner freedom. People are trying to cope with issues of bondage in one form or another. Earlier we talked about bondage versus bonding in human relationships, but there are many other ways in which we have allowed ourselves to become prisoners. For most of us, parts of our spirit become imprisoned as we pass through life— imprisoned by voices from our childhoods still telling us to "try harder," "be the best," "do the most," "win," "be perfect"; imprisoned by our own impossible expectations of ourselves and of others, by our fierce self-sufficiency, by our rigidity and our tendency to take life too seriously, to make it too "heavy," by our inability to relax, to play, to find quiet joy. We forget that our strength is not in doing all and being all, but in surrendering the weight of our load to Christ, who said, "My grace is sufficient for thee: for my strength is made perfect in weakness" (2 Corinthians 12:9).

Oversteering

One way we make our load heavier than it needs to be is by oversteering. When I was a teenager, my brother (four years older than I) got the terrifying task of teaching me to drive. It was wartime, so my dad was overseas, and my mother just knew it would make her too nervous. She was right! I remember that first lesson well. It's a good thing we were out in the country, because I wove all over the gravel road in my attempt to steer. Donal kept saying, "Hey, what're you trying to do, get us both killed? You're oversteering, Twerp!"

Finally, he had me pull over, and he drove, showing me

that it takes only a very slight pressure on the steering wheel to keep the car going along in a straight line. After a few lessons, I got more comfortable in the driver's seat, and gradually let go of my natural tendency to oversteer.

I think that most of us tend to oversteer our way through life, with the same wobbly results. But we don't have to. If we can allow God to take control, the maneuvering becomes less burdensome. *"One of the tasks of life is to learn in some way to give up control—in order to achieve it!"*[1]

In most cases, we tend to overcontrol or oversteer because we had parents who were overly controlling. Somehow, their well-meant efforts to encourage us to succeed were internalized by us as a demand that we be perfect. So we've taken up that cause, expecting the impossible from ourselves. It makes us try too hard—so hard that we become tense and self-condemning. That, of course, defeats our purpose, just as turning the steering wheel too sharply to the left to correct for a slight veering off to the right interferes with our ability to move in a straight, steady line down the highway.

I've found that most of us have an overly controlling inner parent, a voice that keeps telling us we've got to do this, we've got to do that in order to succeed, in order to earn somebody's love, in order to keep up. Sometimes that voice is right on target, but just as often it's playing old tapes that are no longer valid for us. I've found that I need to talk back to my inner parent now and then to keep from taking myself too seriously.

For example, having guests for dinner was always hard for me. I'd wear myself out cleaning the house, washing every window, moving every piece of furniture, dusting the tops of door frames, sweeping the sidewalk, and many other nonessential tasks, because there was an unspoken rule in my head that the house had to be absolutely spotless for company. By the time I did the grocery shopping, polished the silver, ironed the linen tablecloth and napkins, and cooked my fanciest recipes, I'd be too worn out to enjoy my guests. But of course, I couldn't serve on placemats, or use the everyday dishes, or fix simple meals, could I? After all, there was that inner parent who kept telling me it all had to be perfect in order to be a success. No wonder I gradually entertained less and less!

Lately, though, I've been talking back to that voice that demands perfection. I'm deliberately making statements such as, "So *what* if I miss a cobweb, or the pie doesn't set, or the meat is a little overcooked? Are my friends coming to inspect my housekeeping or test my cooking ability? Of course not!" I'm still rather uneasy about entertaining. I know there are other things I do better. But the meals I fix for company are getting simpler and simpler, and I'm actually beginning to enjoy the whole process.

In the interest of easy steering, pay attention to those unexamined rules in your head, those parental voices that sometimes govern you in outmoded ways. Begin to question your inner script. Listen to what you're telling yourself. You may find that oversteering is making your load unnecessarily heavy.

Expecting the Impossible of Ourselves

Another way we overload ourselves as we travel through life is by setting up expectations that are either unrealistic or downright impossible. For instance, many of us think (consciously or unconsciously) that we must be everything to everybody. Married women with children and careers are particularly prone to this, although many men also find themselves trying to live out impossible expectations.

Dan (name changed) is in his late thirties, has his own business, is married and the father of three small children. His career is quite successful because Dan has always worked twelve hours a day, including weekends, except for Sundays, which he spends doing something special with his family. His wife works, too, so Dan tried to help Deb with the housework after he got home from the office, usually around ten or eleven at night. He did all the cooking on Sundays.

This family is greatly admired by all who know them, and they've always appeared to be extremely happy. Early last summer, though, Dan crashed into a depression so black that he tried to kill himself. Fortunately, his attempt was not successful (one of the few failures in Dan's life). Hospitalization and intense psychotherapy helped this young man to see that he had set up impossible standards for himself. Since then, the family has moved into a smaller, less expensive home, relieving them of their heavy financial burden. They've also hired a woman to clean once a week and to cook for them on weekends. Both Dan and Deb are enjoying a new sense of freedom they've not known for years.

"It was really hard to let go," says Dan. "I felt so *responsible*. But all of this has shown me that I can't be any good to anyone else unless I can be good to myself, too. I'm really thankful this happened!" Dan has learned to let go of his impossible expectations of himself.

Many of us who have careers have an inner drive to reach the top in our field. But have you ever stopped to think what that means? Where *is* the top? There's *no such place*. Every goal achieved offers another to strive toward, doesn't it? The view from the top of the mountain always reveals other peaks to be climbed. This has been true since the world began.

Impossible expectations are not limited to our outward actions, though. Sometimes we expect the impossible from ourselves emotionally, too. Do you think you should always feel loving toward your spouse, your children, or your friends? Even if your answer to that question is no, you may unconsciously expect it of yourself.

I always wanted to be a perfect mother, and I actually believed such a thing was possible. When my babies cried, I picked them up immediately, and if feeding and changing didn't calm them, I rocked them and walked the floor with them until they finally fell asleep and I fell into bed exhausted. I'm not sorry I did that. I'd do it again. The only thing wrong was that I couldn't admit to myself that I sometimes felt irritated about it, that I really didn't always want to do it, that I sometimes resented having to get up in the middle of the night. Yet all of those feelings were perfectly normal human reactions. What I've since discovered is that, even when you consciously deny your negative feelings, something inside of you knows they're there. The result? In my case, it was a lot of vague feelings of guilt that hinted to me that I must surely be a failure as a mother.

I'm still a little afraid of my own anger. It's not "nice" to be angry, and I was brought up to be a "nice girl." But I've at least learned to recognize my own negative feelings and to try to deal with them. I'll probably never be the kind who yells and screams, but I can write out my anger in my journal and offer it to God. I can take a brisk walk, and more and more often I'm able to be assertive when it's necessary. I think I've finally given up the impossible expectation that I should always feel loving toward those I care about. If I can accept myself, shadows and all, the humanity of Jesus can then restore me to a relationship with His Father that I do not deserve. And this is the incredible grace of it: that out of the honesty of claimed darkness, a love named Christ can rise in my life like the sun, erasing the night.

Expecting the Impossible of Others

Not only do we tend to place impossible demands upon ourselves, but we also do it to others. One way this often comes out is in looking for the perfect mate. Magazines that cater to young women are full of articles about how to find "Mr. Right," and, once he's found, how to snag him. Many movies and TV shows present the unrealistic notion that there is an ideal mate for each person. Of course, we all know (at least intellectually) that there is no such thing as a perfect husband or wife. There are only flawed human beings.

My Aunt Alta, who was a third-grade schoolteacher in Omaha for thirty years, never married, because my grandfather thought that none of the young men she dated was good enough for her. In this day of independence, what Papa thinks might not make that much difference. Still, many single people do expect to find someone who fits all their qualifications. What happens then is that they either give up the idea of committing to any long-term relationship, or they convince themselves that the person they've "fallen in love with" really does have all the qualities they desire in a mate. The latter is by far the worst choice of the two, because it is not love. It is simply the projection of one's own unrealistic ideals onto the other person. The "gods" we create by such expectations are no better than the heathen idols condemned by the Old Testament prophets—sure to let us down. (See Isaiah 40:18–20; 44:9–20.) Idolizing also encourages a prospective mate to hide who he or she really is, in an effort to fit into the other person's mold. Of course, in a good marriage both partners need to make adjustments, but trying to force yourself into someone else's mold, or forcing someone else into your mold, is being untrue to the self God created you to be.

Eugene Kennedy has written some important words about being faithful to our own true selves:

> There is a living and invisible force that is generated by faithfulness within ourselves that weathers and strengthens us like a warming sun. This is the heart of stable truth about ourselves which others can touch and sense as reliable and trustworthy. . . . We have to hold on to that fundamental truth that springs from a good sense of ourselves or we cannot even recognize much less share who we are with anybody else.[2]

Yoked with God, we can allow ourselves—and others—to be the unique persons God created and to celebrate our differences . . . another reminder of the yoke that frees.

But it's not only in our search for a mate that we put impossible expectations on others. Most parents have dreams for their children, in which they are successful in all phases of life. They must excel academically as well in extracurricular activities, and, of course, they must also be popular. Then they must have successful careers, active social lives, spouses the parents like, and finally (to come full circle) happy, well-adjusted children. There's certainly nothing wrong with these parental goals. The only trouble is that such impossible expectations of perfection are likely to backfire, causing our children to feel like failures and us as parents to feel disillusioned when our hopes and dreams aren't fully met. How important it is for us parents to learn the lesson of easy steering.

A similar situation occurs for us when we hope to find the perfect friend—one who shares all of our interests, who can fulfill all of our social and personal needs not met at home. There was a time in my life when I was looking for just such a person. What I was really searching for, of course, was another me. (Thank goodness I didn't find one. I probably couldn't have stood her!)

I now think I've found the perfect friend. But guess what? My friend is a composite. Outside of my family, Jan is the one with whom I share my deepest self. But I also need Carolmae who prays with me, and Cheri whose personality type is similar to mine, and Sarah whose strength and sound advice have helped me through some tough times, and Eugene who shares my love of simplicity and silence. Anita's wonderful sense of humor keeps me from taking myself too seriously, Bill sparks my intellect, Betty Jo and Dorothy's friendships give me a sense of continuity, and Carol shares my interest in writing. There are others, too. Once I gave up the idea of finding all those qualities in one person, I found my "perfect friend" in several much-loved people.

This shift in perspective has also made me realize that *I* cannot be the one perfect friend for anyone, because it is impossible for me to fill all of another's needs. It's helping me to be less possessive of the special people in my life. Again, Eugene Kennedy says it well: "The more we want each other, the more we must be willing to respect each other's separateness. The more we would be sensitive to each other's needs, the more we must be willing to let each other go."[3]

Carrying God on Our Backs

We expect the impossible of ourselves and of others because we don't expect *enough* of God. In a sermon entitled "God on Our Backs," Edmund Steimle called attention to the ludicrous scene in Isaiah 46, in which the Babylonians are retreating with their load-bearing beasts carrying the gods of the people on their backs.

How could those people have thought there could be any power in gods that had to be carried on the backs of animals? Yet, as Steimle points out, many of us act as though we think we have to carry God. What we're really carrying is a heavy load of guilt. Going to church becomes a chore—a duty— and we think it's only because of our tithes and offerings that the church is saved from being swept away. Do we really believe that the holiness and riches of God's mercy depend on *us?* Everything connected with God becomes deadly serious business. We have a "lurking suspicion that God's really against us and has to be bought off so we won't have bad luck, sickness, tragedy."

If our faith is more of a burden than a lift, Steimle says, something is wrong. Of course, there *is* work to be done. We do need to take up the yoke. But we don't have to bear the load alone. Jesus' yoke is *easy.* His burden is *light.* "God is not behind us squelching us. He is ahead of us, always beckoning. If God really is for us (and He really is, no matter how it looks), our burdens are indeed light."[4]

Steimle concludes with this passage from Isaiah 46:3–4:

> Harken to me, O house of Jacob, all the remnant of the house of Israel, who have been borne by me from your birth, carried from the womb; even to your old age I am He, and to gray hairs I will carry you. I have made, and I will bear; I will carry and will save.[5]

If you're feeling weighed down today, think of those Babylonians lugging their heavy metal gods, and give thanks for our load-lightening God who is not weighing us down but standing ready to lift as much of our load as we're willing to give Him.

Letting God Pull the Load

As we've seen in the previous chapters, all the graces of life are dependent not on what human beings do but on what God does. During those times we're truly *yoked with God,* He does the pulling of the load. He provides the power, the direction, and the stability we need in order to move steadily forward.

One of my first experiences with this occurred a few years ago, when I was just beginning to lead retreats. For each retreat I not only spent a great amount of time preparing, but I fretted and stewed quite a bit during the preparatory time. It seemed to be such a heavy responsibility. I think that sometimes I actually over prepared, so that my presentations became somewhat self-conscious and even a little rigid.

Then, just as I began to prepare for a weekend workshop in Omaha, I got the flu. I was in bed for nearly a week, and suddenly there was almost no time left to work out what I was going to say in my talks. The theme for the weekend was one I'd never addressed before. Should I call and cancel? Somehow, I just couldn't. When I prayed about it, I sensed that God wanted me to learn to trust Him, so I made the decision to go ahead. (A theme that recurs often in my dreams is being unprepared for some occasion and making an absolute fool of myself. Now here I was, about to live out that nightmare!) My only preparation time was the night before, plus the time on the airplane.

The night before I got absolutely nowhere. I read relevant Scripture passages and some commentaries and then sat at my typewriter and stared at the blank page until midnight, when I gave up and went to bed. As I pulled up the covers, I told God that since He seemed to want me to do this, He'd have to provide whatever I needed.

Suddenly, I seemed to hear God say, "Who's in control here, anyway?"

The question startled me, but the moment I answered, "You are!" I felt something let go inside of me, like an elastic tourniquet being released. I was amazed that I fell right to sleep and woke up refreshed. On the airplane, ideas started flooding into me. I grabbed my notebook and could hardly write fast enough. In the short time I had, all I could do was to jot down a few notes. (Normally I have my talks written out and practically memorized.)

All the way into the city in the taxi, and then as I walked to the podium, and finally, just before I began to speak, I replayed in my mind those words from the night before. "Who's in control here, anyway?" And I tried to answer, as confidently as possible, *"You* are!"

I really did feel as though the Holy Spirit took over and gave me the words to say, just as Jesus told the disciples He would (Matthew 10:19). It was a good retreat. Maybe better than any I'd led before. I think it was a turning point.

I don't mean to imply that preparation is unnecessary. I have never "winged it" so completely since. (Doesn't that give new meaning to the metaphor, *winging it?* With whose wings? *We* know!) Anyway, my Omaha experience has helped to change my attitude, my whole feeling about the assignments God gives me. I can walk lightly now, knowing that I have a partner, sensing His presence, trusting His grace to bear me up.

When responsibility is heavy on you, perhaps it would help you to close your eyes for just long enough to hear God's question, "Who's in control here, anyway?" and to answer, *"You* are!" It can make your burden lighter.

Praying It by Ear

A frequently used cliché in our family is, "Well, let's just play it by ear," meaning that we'll decide things as they come up. We'll go with the flow, doing what seems right at the moment. Sometimes this works out well, but often it doesn't. I've decided that, for me at least, it's much better to plan ahead to whatever extent I can.

There are always times, however, in which planning ahead is simply not possible. "How easy it is to get overwrought and frustrated if we are trying to live by a perfectly planned-out schedule that leaves no room for interruptions or the natural inclination of things and schedules to break down. If we depend on our planning, we're not really depending on God!"[6] I think we need to plan to whatever extent the situation allows, and then offer that plan to God, keeping our agenda open-ended, trusting Him to help us handle whatever comes up.

A few years ago, a friend who was facing a day of great uncertainty said, "Well, I guess I'll just have to pray it by ear." I thought I'd heard wrong, but when I asked what she meant by that, she said that she begins each day by thanking God for her life and offering it back to Him to use as He will. In addition to that, praying it by ear for me means *listening* prayer. I need to present myself to God, offer my day or my problem to Him, and then stop my incessant inner chatter long enough to listen to Him. It means that my prayer needs to continue, without words, even after my scheduled time with God is past. The way it continues is by a listening attitude, by staying tuned to God's station as I go through the day, by being aware of His inner leadings, and by having the courage to follow them. I know this is a big order, and I confess that I'm rarely able to do it fully, but I've been helped by my friend's way of praying. Here's my adaptation of her prayer:

> *Heavenly Father, I thank You for this day and offer it back to You. At this moment, I acknowledge the insepa-rable connection between us, the yoke. I know I'll forget about it sometimes, probably when I need You most, so I'm asking You ahead of time to stay in control, through*

*all of the decisions, interactions, and possibilities in the
hours and minutes ahead. Guide me even when I forget
that You are my Partner. You know all my faults and
flaws, my blocks, hangups, rebellions and self-doubts.
Steer me around, through, or in spite of them, Lord.
Help me to "pray it by ear" all day, in the name of Jesus.*

Amen.

I have seen a big contrast between the days when I've
started with this prayer and the days when I've forgotten. It's
not a magic formula for a smooth and happy day, nor a way
to manipulate God. Problems come up whether I've started
my day the pray-it-by-ear way or not. Hard decisions have
to be made. Yet very often, at the heart of a crisis, I remember that I've asked God to stay in control, and that tourniquet inside of me lets go. I think it frees me to make wiser
decisions, to relate to difficult people better, to see my own
errors and to correct them.

Paul Welter, who is a college professor, counselor, writer,
and a prayerful man, says that creativity is the willingness to
be out of control. Here's an example he gives:

I have discovered in teaching, writing, and counseling
that the real transformations occur when I become willing to let go of a plan, to give up control, to grasp an
unexpected new initiative. A young woman worked
through great pain in counseling concerning the many
kinds of abuse she had suffered as a child. But she still
was walking into life with her head turned to the past.
Finally the session came when I reached the end of my
skills. She came the next time with two paintings—the
first a vivid representation of the rage and depression
she felt at the present, and the second a beautiful, peaceful pastoral scene that represented the person she
wanted to become. We talked for a couple of sessions
about these paintings. Then one spring day when she
was by herself in a meadow much like the one she had
drawn, she had a spiritual experience in which she
walked through the bad painting and into the good one.
I had no control of that moment. Perhaps she, too, lost
some control of her own life and found freedom from

the bondage of her past. When I could no longer visualize how her healing would occur, it came as a gift from God.[7]

But sometimes I *intend* to "pray it by ear" and then later realize that I've grabbed back my control and forgotten all about letting God run the show. At times like that, it helps to have some quick way of reminding yourself of your connection with God, as the day goes by. It may be just to close your eyes for a moment, or to look at the sky, to put your hand over your heart, or simply to cry, "God, help!" A man I know connects with Christ by touching the cross he carries in his pocket. If you can find a simple way of reminding yourself of your connection with God, it will help you let go of your control so He can lighten your load.

Carrying Our Load with Open Hands

Maybe you've heard the story about the monkey who couldn't get the nuts out of the box with the hand-sized hole in it because his fist, full of nuts, kept getting caught on its way out of the box. All he'd have had to do was to open his hand a little. He might have lost a few peanuts, but at least he would have had *some!*

Clench your fists for a moment, and then open your hands. Can you feel the tension leaving? The open hand is a wonderful symbol for achieving control by giving it up to God. Open hands are a symbol of peace. It takes an open, unclenched hand to plant a garden, paint a picture, perform surgery. Only an open hand can clasp another person's hand, give a child a pat on the back, type a letter, turn the pages of a book, lift a baby, pet a dog.

The open hand is a receptive hand, a picture of the soul that is open to God. When I open my hands and lift them to Him, I am empowered, so that I can say with Jesus, "I can of mine own self do nothing . . . but the Father that dwelleth in me, he doeth the works" (John 5:30 and 14:10).

Open hands also remind me of the fact that every creative act is performed, not by trying, but by letting. As you know, God creates by letting. "Let there be light . . . Let there be a firmament . . . Let the earth bring forth grass . . ." (Genesis

1:3, 6, 11). God said "let" at every act of creation. At some point in every *human* creative act, it is necessary to *let* go, to allow what is beyond us to come into being. If we can *let* God, He will.

I'd like to close with some excerpts from a description of letting go that I found in my files.

Letting Go

Letting go does not mean to stop caring;
    It means I can't do it for someone else.
Letting go is not to cut myself off;
    It's the realization I can't control another.
Letting go is to admit powerlessness,
    Which means the outcome is not in my hands.
Letting go is not to try to change another;
    It's to make the most of myself.
Letting go is not to dwell in past regrets
    But to grow and live for the future.
Letting go is to fear less and live more.

—Anonymous

Our Lord's yoke is easy, and His burden is light, because He bears it for us. When two animals are yoked together, the weaker one needs only to get in step with the stronger, and his burden, no matter how heavy it has been, will become light. It is the same for you and me.

NOTES

1. William F. Nerin, *Family Reconstruction: Long Day's Journey into Light* (New York: W.W. Norton, 1986), p. 141.

2. Eugene Kennedy, *The Joy of Being Human* (Garden City, N.Y.: Image Books, 1976), p. 285.

3. *Ibid.,* p. 287.

4. Edmund Steimle in a sermon delivered at the National Association of Teachers of Music, Montreat, North Carolina, July 29, 1976.

5. *Ibid.*

6. Mary Ruth Howes, in a letter to the author, February 8, 1989.

7. Paul Welter, "The Gift of Creativity—The Willingness to Be Out of Control," *Faith at Work* (November/December, 1987), p. 4.

CHAPTER 9

The Gift of a Peaceful Spirit

Peace I bequeath to you, my own peace I give you, a peace
the world cannot give, this is my gift to you.

John 14:27, JB

As I was thinking about the gift of a peaceful spirit,
a story formed in my mind. Perhaps it could be called a
parable.

A young man named Jason had been searching all of his
life for peace and had not found it, so he went to visit a wise
old man who lived in a hut by the river. "Please," he said,
"can you tell me how to find peace?"

The old man told Jason that he could and surely would
help him, but first Jason would have to bring him three
things: an ear of corn grown by his own efforts; two pieces
of wood made from a tree he'd cut down, sawn into planks,
and sanded to smoothness; and a live, white-winged dove.
Then he gave the young man three corn seeds and sent him
on his way.

Jason was disappointed because he wanted peace *now.*
Still, he decided to give it a try, because without peace, life
did not seem worth living. It was almost a year before Jason
returned to the hut. Bent over under the weight of the heavy
planks he carried on his back, he trudged up to where his

mentor stood, dropped the wood and his satchel on the ground, and fell in a heap beside them.

"I've failed," he moaned. "I give up. There is no peace."

The old man sat on the ground beside him and asked what had happened. Jason reached into his satchel and pulled out an ear of corn.

"I've brought the corn," said the younger man, "but it doesn't count, because I didn't grow it solely by my own efforts. It's true that I planted it and watered it and cut down the weeds around it. But after I did all of that, I realized that there was nothing more I could do, so I just sat and waited. Day after day, the sun shone on it, through no effort of mine, and finally a sprout came out of the ground. It was very clear to me then: *I* did not make it happen."

The older man stroked his bushy white beard and then placed his gnarled hand on the young man's shoulder. "Well done," he said. "You have discovered the first secret of peace: God the Father is Your only power."

Then Jason began to tell the old man about his struggle with the second task, which was much harder than the first. He'd quickly found a large tree to fell, but when he asked permission to chop it down, the owner of the land became very angry and chased him off his property. This was repeated again and again with other landowners, until the young man was ready to give up. He had walked a long way, and his feet were blistered. Just when he was sure he could go no farther, he saw another house in the distance, surrounded by woodlands. "I'll try once more," he thought, "and then I'll give up on finding peace."

This time, the landowner asked what the young man could pay. Searching in his satchel, he took out an ear of corn and told the man he could have all its seeds and the crop that grew from them. In this way, he got permission. Working with an ax and saw borrowed from the landowner, he found a sturdy tree and began to chop and saw. It was much harder work than he'd expected, but he kept on until the tree finally fell, knocking him over and injuring his left foot. The next day, limping and exhausted, he split the tree lengthwise, so that he now had two boards. Then he looked around until he found a rough piece of granite with which to smooth the wood. It took him weeks to finish.

"By that time," said Jason, "my hands were bleeding, but I lifted the heavy wood onto my back and trudged all these many miles back to your hut. This was the most difficult thing I've ever done in my life," said the young man. "And for what? The planks are ruined. Just look at the wood and you'll see that blood from my hands and feet has stained the wood. What good are these to anyone?"

The old man placed the shorter piece of wood across the longer one and nailed them together at the point where they crossed. Then he gave the younger man a cool drink of water and said, "Well done, my son. You have discovered the second secret of a peaceful heart: Face your pain head-on and see it through. Like God the Son, peace often comes nailed to a cross."

Jason heaved a heavy sigh and said, "But I have absolutely and completely failed the third test. In all of my searching, I found only two white-winged doves. I tried taming them, trapping them, chasing them, everything I could, but it was all useless. They eluded me every time. Maybe I was just not meant to find peace. I am going to give up the search."

At that moment, there was a rustling in the tall trees over the heads of the two men, and a gloriously beautiful bird with an iridescent breast spread its white wings and glided softly down, landing gently on Jason's left shoulder, just above his heart.

"Well done, my son," said the old man. "Now you know the third secret of peace: You cannot find it. It must find you. Like God the Holy Spirit, peace descends like a dove on the surrendered heart.

"Those three secrets are all you need to learn about peace," said the old man.

"Know that God is your only power.
"Face your pain head-on and see it through.
"Surrender your heart, and peace will find you."

God Is Your Only Power

Like Jason, I've had to learn, again and again, the lesson of the growing corn: that God is my only power. I know it in my head, of course, but my heart keeps forgetting. Or perhaps it's my ego that forgets. I know I've forgotten when:

It's 10:00 A.M. and my work isn't going well and I suddenly remember that I neglected to start the morning by asking for God's help; or when I've been losing sleep worrying about the problems of one of my grown children, as if it were up to me to fix everything; or when financial insecurity causes me to get tightfisted instead of openhandedly trusting my Source. At times like these, I need to remind myself that it's *not* all up to me. In fact, I have no power. None whatever. Only God's power can make my work right, or solve my children's problems, or provide for my material needs. If I can remind myself of this every day, whenever my peace of mind is threatened by frustration, worry, or fear, I can begin to let go.

Power to Change Lives

As I was trying to decide which Scriptural illustration to cite as evidence of God's power in the face of human power-lessness, my mind was flooded with examples: Abraham and Sarah giving birth in their old age; Jacob wrestling with the angel and being blessed with a new name and a fresh start; manna in the desert when the food ran out; water from a rock when thirst was unbearable; the walls of Jericho tumbling down; all the healing miracles of Jesus. These are only a few of the many evidences of God's ability to work wonders, after human beings have given up.

Twice as I was thinking about these displays of power, the incident of Jesus' meeting with the Samaritan woman at the well came into my mind, and twice I dismissed it as not applicable. But the third time it happened, I decided to pay attention. Then I saw it! The greatest evidences of God's power are not in pillars of fire, or parted seas, or defeated armies, but in His power to change the human heart. The final issue is not material, but spiritual. As a result of her brief meeting with Jesus at the well, this Samaritan woman who had made a complete mess of her life was miraculously transformed into a living, joyous, radiant example of the power of the Spirit (John 4:5–14). We know this because she accepted Him as the Messiah and immediately went about the village telling everyone that good news.

Like the Samaritan woman, I sometimes feel that I've

made a hopeless mess of my life. Don't we all have those feelings sometimes? When it happens to me, my inclination is to try to take control and "straighten things out." More often than not, I make matters worse. But if I can call on God's power instead, His promise of Isaiah 45 is fulfilled: "I will go before thee, and make the crooked places straight: I will break in pieces the gates of brass, and cut in sunder the bars of iron" (Isaiah 45:2). That's power—God's power—the power that brings inner peace.

Here's something to think about: whenever we attempt to accomplish anything by personal force, we have to *maintain* it by personal force! When we let up, the power goes out of it. Haven't we each proved our own powerlessness, at least to ourselves? On the other hand, when we truly offer it to God and then follow *His* leadings, all the powers of the universe come to our aid! If you can hold this truth in your heart, you will have all the power you will ever need for every good thing in your life, and you will truly receive "grace heaped upon grace" (John 1:16, NEB).

The clue to doing this is in the story of the woman at the well. She came there *every day* for water. Think what might have happened if she had missed that one day! Our part is to set aside a reasonable time each day for prayer, Bible reading, and listening; then to try to live in accordance with God's will, *as far as is possible for us at the moment.* If we're sincerely doing this, we can give ourselves permission to let go of all the results, trusting the outcome to God. Only then can *His* power take over. Only then can His peace be ours.

Power That Brings Order Out of Chaos

So how can we tell whether or not God's power is at work in our lives? One distinguishing characteristic of His actions is *orderliness.* From the creation of an ordered universe out of a chaotic, formless void, to His plan for the salvation of the peoples of the earth through the death and resurrection of His Son, God has and always will proceed in ordered ways. "He hath made with me an everlasting covenant, ordered in all things, and sure" (2 Samuel 23:5). Order and power go together. In fact, French philosopher Henri Frederic Amiel wrote: "Order *is* power." And Paul, in his first letter to the Corinthians, urged those who would follow Christ to "let all things be done decently and in order" (14:40).

Order is one of the natural attributes of God and therefore of the human spirit. Allowing *God's orderliness* to come into the chaotic aspects of our lives is an essential part of a peaceful spirit. This can happen from the inside out (by regularly centering ourselves in Christ and letting that peace fan out into all we do) or from the outside in.

I'm an introvert, so I more often choose the inside-out way of inviting God to restore His order in my life when my peace of mind has flown. When I do this regularly, subtle changes begin to happen. A little at a time, the clutter on my desk begins to disappear. Parts of my life that had become too crowded start to clear. Tangles in relationships smooth out like newly combed hair. This is not to say that no problems arise. *If I'm faithful to that center,* though, there is a quiet pool within that helps to order my outer world. I believe Shakespeare's words, "We do not keep the outward form of order, where there is deep disorder in the mind."[1] Since we've discussed solitude and centering in an earlier chapter, we won't go into it again here, except to say that time alone with God plants seeds of peace in our hearts.

But I know that some people can't stand to sit for more than a minute or two, and others honestly can't find the time. What can we do, then, to bring order into our lives from the outside? We can learn to focus on one thing at a time. Here's an experience shared with me by a friend:

> For me, focus means that I should open the mail at my desk and file everything or take care of it right away instead of what I do do—open and read the mail right after I walk in the door from work while I take off my boots and feed the cat and turn on the TV and change my clothes and begin to fix something to eat. And there is the mail strewn from front hall to kitchen table to bathroom—and none of it at my desk!![2]

Can't we all identify with that? I certainly can. Perhaps we could excerpt Paul's words of Philippians 3:14 and put them to work for us: "This one thing I do." If we'd place those words as reminders in strategic places, maybe we could stay more focused on one thing at a time. For example, my friend might tape them onto the inside of her mailbox, where she'd see them when she takes out her mail. As they remind her of her mission as a Christian, they could also be a call for singlemindedness in handling the mail. She could let them be a cue to walk straight to her desk, sit down, and read the mail, decide what to do with each piece, and either do what needs to be done or file it for processing later. It could be a way of bringing Christ with His orderliness into everyday life.

Have you ever found yourself wasting time, even when you have a lot to do? Think about it! I think it happens when we're so overwhelmed by all the things we need to do that our sense of order gets thrown off and we start stumbling around instead of moving forward. Last fall, I found myself with a whole bushel of work assignments to complete before the end of the year, as well as several special occasions to prepare for. It seemed impossible. I noticed myself getting tense and anxious and accomplishing little.

From other times when this has happened, I've learned that I can handle it *all, if I can get a sense of order going for me.* I can get unstuck by making a list, offering it to God, and then doing just *one thing* from that list. So I took my calendar and assigned one portion of the work to each week. As I did this, I could see that there really was time to do it all, if I kept to my schedule. I typed it up, ran extra copies, and taped them up where I'd see them at switch points of the day, such as right after breakfast, as soon as I came into my office, and just before bed. Each time I looked at my schedule, I offered it to God. Though there were times when I fell behind, just having an orderly plan took away the feeling of being overwhelmed, as I checked off the weeks and kept after it. I was able to meet all my deadlines, including getting ready for twenty Thanksgiving dinner guests and doing the family Christmas shopping. Even more important than that, order gave me the priceless grace of peace of mind through it all.

Peace Comes Nailed to a Cross

Claiming the gift of peace of mind is not always peaceful, however. This has been one of the hardest lessons of my life, and I'm still working on it. Like Jason, I thought I could find peace if I asked wise people and practiced spiritual disciplines. Those things help, of course—but it's in the day-in, day-out struggles of life that the deeper peace is won. Maybe some of the hard lessons of my life will be helpful to you.

Stop Trying to Avoid Conflict

I had to learn that *avoiding conflict does not bring peace; it increases turmoil.* The same Jesus who promised me a peace the world could not give (John 14:27) also said that He came to bring me a sword (Matthew 10:34). This seems to be a contradiction, but my own struggles have shown me that it is not.

In the past, when difficult situations arose in my life, I tended to say to myself, "Oh well. Things could be worse," or, "I'd better not rock the boat." Or else I tried to distract myself by getting very busy, hoping irrationally that the problems would go away. Now, seeing that written down, it appears quite ridiculous, doesn't it? And yet it's an unconscious tendency for many people, particularly those who grew up in homes where anger was not an acceptable emotion, or in homes in which there was a great amount of conflict that was frightening to the child.

All of us have *some* tendency to avoid facing unpleasant situations. For example, there's that difficult phone call in which you have to ask for something, tell someone news you know they don't want to hear, or admit you've forgotten to do something they asked and now it's too late. These situations come up for all of us. Or there's the decision that is a double bind. Either way you choose, someone's feelings will be hurt. I've always tended to put off things like that. The result is that, instead of interfering with my peace of mind for ten minutes (as it would if I made the phone call immediately or came to a prompt decision), it blocks my serenity for several days because, even though I may lay a blanket of busyness over it, it continues to gnaw away inside of me. Besides that, more often than not, the delay makes things worse. Postponement of issues often results in remarks such as, "Why didn't you say so right away?" or, "But if you'd just told me sooner, I could have. . . ."

Indecision and avoidance of issues and problems destroy peace of mind, not the way a tornado destroys buildings but the way termites do—persistently and below the surface.

A while back, my brother called to make a request about the family farm we own together. I said I'd have to think about it and get back to him. After I had considered the situation, I could see that I really needed to say no to his request. But I dreaded telling him. Oh, how I dreaded it.

I was having company that evening, so I excused myself from making the call that day. Yet as I prepared for my guests, I worried about what I'd say and what Donal would say, fully expecting him to be angry and fearing that anger. My fear made me tense and nervous. I kept dropping things, forgetting to turn on the timer for baking, having to make extra trips to the store because my mind had been on the dreaded phone call while I shopped. It seemed to me that even my guests picked up my tension, because our conversation was rather strained. I was completely exhausted after they left and didn't sleep well that night, still worrying about the call.

The next day, when I finally called my brother he was really quite understanding. In fact, he was *glad* I'd brought up an issue he'd never thought about. After I hung up the phone, I laughed at myself, realizing that I could have avoided so much distress if I'd just made the phone call the day before! Even if his response had been angry, it would have been better to have *that* out in the open sooner, so it could be dealt with before it grew by being held in.

That is only a small instance of how avoidance of a difficult situation can ruin one's peace of mind. But, like Jason, I'm beginning to see that facing the tough stuff *as it comes up* and seeing it through is a very important key to a peaceful heart. Martin Luther King said it so well: "Courage faces fear and thereby masters it. Cowardice represses fear and is thereby mastered by it."[3]

Let Your Pain Be Pain

Charlotte Davis Kasl has written that much of our distress in life is due to the fact that we are afraid to know what we know, afraid to let our pain be pain.[4] Both fears, once they're faced, are bearable. What does it mean to be afraid to know what you know? A young friend of mine (we'll call her Susan) had an unconscious fear that she didn't really love her husband. Because she couldn't admit that to herself, she overcompensated by trying constantly to please him, no matter what the cost to her sense of personal worth. Yet each time she gave up part of herself, resentment between them grew. When Susan became physically ill, her doctor was finally able to break through and help her to know what she knew. Facing her fear head-on, she saw that she had not failed as a wife. Counseling brought the couple into a more honest relationship. They are now tearing down that wall, brick by brick. They'll make it, though their peace comes nailed to a cross.

Let your pain be pain. That's good advice. I know it physically, from giving birth to three children. To whatever extent you resist your pain, it will worsen. But if you *go with it,* somehow the seemingly unbearable becomes at least tolerable. It's the same with emotional pain. If you resist it, sit on it, try to pretend it isn't there, ignore it, or run away from it, it will almost surely increase. However, if you walk right into it, you'll soon find yourself coming out on the other side. And in the process, a new, stronger you may be born!

Learn to Walk Through Pain

How, then, can I walk into and through my emotional pain in order to receive the gift of a peaceful spirit? One of the best possible helps I've found is to talk it out with a trusted friend. If you have someone who will truly listen to you without judging, without giving advice unless you ask for it, without stealing the conversation, you have a jewel worth more than many diamonds. ("Stealing the conversation"[5] means saying something like, "Oh, I know what you mean. That happened to me just the other day . . . " and then switching the conversation to their own problems, leaving you sitting there holding your pain.) Of course, sharing must be a two-way thing. But it's important, with close friends, to stay with the one who is hurting until they've had a chance to get out all the pain. *Then* the one who's been talking can truly listen to the other. Jan and I have found that sometimes one of us needs to talk more, and sometimes the other's pain is greater.

Other things that have helped me face emotional pain are: writing out my feelings in my journal, going for a brisk walk, or screaming into a pillow. I've also discovered that, when I can't do any of the above, I can go into the bedroom or other private place and have a "silent scream." This means taking a deep breath, tensing every muscle in my body, and expelling the air forcefully, continuing to push it out even after it seems to be all gone. Try it sometime, especially when you're feeling angry. You may be amazed at the rush of relief that follows a silent scream or two. The reason why all of these *physical* things are important is that, when you feel strong emotion, your body releases chemicals into your bloodstream that were originally meant to give you the strength to do physical battle, or to run away fast. Of course, these fight-or-flight options are seldom used now, but the chemicals are still secreted. If they aren't "worked off" physically, they build up, causing further stress and sometimes even illness.

Nurture Your Inner Child

Another way of facing pain is to deal with your inner child. Have you ever had a strong emotion come over you that you couldn't figure out? Maybe it's an overreaction to something someone else said or did. Your feelings are hurt, and suddenly you're in tears or wanting to withdraw, or else you're in a rage that's all out of proportion to the event, and your peace of mind has been completely shattered. When such things happen to me, I ask myself what part of me that's coming from. Very often, it's my inner, hurt child. All of us have hurts left over from childhood, and they can ambush us when we least expect it.

Just a few days ago, a friend said something that hurt my feelings. Normally it wouldn't have been a big deal, but that little kid in me got into the act, and before long, she had blown it all out of proportion to the actual circumstances. I found myself in tears, so I got my journal and went to my quiet place. Then I asked that hurt child what she wanted from me. Immediately the response came, "I just want to know I'm lovable."

So *that* was why she was having such a fit! I tried to think about how I could give my inner child what she wanted, and I decided to write her a letter. In it, I expressed my appreciation for all of the childlike qualities she gifts me with, such as creativity and a sense of wonder. I even thanked her for her tears, knowing that they increase my sensitivity to the pain of others. All of this must have been exactly what she wanted from me, because she calmed down, and my peace of mind returned.

"There is no part of you," Gordon Scott writes, "that will not transform into gift—positive and light—if you accept, talk with, work with it. Grace is a nurturing connection between the conscious and the unconscious."[6] If you are in the throes of a painful emotion, ask yourself if it could be your inner child acting up. If so, ask her what she wants. Then, instead of giving her negative messages, such as "I must be an awful person to feel this way," try giving her what she wants and isn't getting from others at the moment.

All of these are ways to let our pain be pain instead of numbing or running from it. They can help us to find the deeper peace that comes only from facing our pain head-on and seeing it through. They bring the peace of the conquered cross.

Surrender Your Heart

Like Jason, who found that peace could not be trapped, tamed, or forced, there comes a point in the search for peace at which I need to just let go and surrender my heart to the Holy Spirit. I need to give up trying to find peace, so that the peace of Christ can find me.

By Giving Thanks

I know this intellectually, but I often find myself turning my worries and concerns over to God and then taking them back the next day, or the next hour. Do you ever find it hard to stop your mind from dwelling on the negative? A few weeks ago, I had one of the most frightening experiences of my life. I was driving to the post office when a boy on a bicycle made a sudden left turn right in front of my car. I slammed on the brakes but was unable to stop in time to avoid hitting him. He went up over the hood of my car, hitting his head on my windshield so hard it broke the glass.

There's no way I can describe the horror of that moment. I can still hear the sound, still see the shocked look on his face as he hit the glass. I jumped out of the car, terrified of what I might find. What I did find was a very brave ten-year-old named Seth Hendrickson already getting up and brushing himself off. He was *all right!* I could hardly believe it.

Even though the policeman kept telling me it was not my fault (Seth made the sudden turn on a dare from a friend, and my skid marks indicated I wasn't speeding), I couldn't let go of the incident. Seth was taken to the hospital, thoroughly examined and released, but I was still emotionally shaken. In all the years I'd been driving, I'd often thought there could be nothing worse than to hit a child. Now it had happened. The scene kept replaying in my mind. I'd wake up in the night thinking about it, filled with dread about what *might* have happened. (What if he'd broken his neck? What if he'd fractured his skull and had brain damage? What if, instead of going over the hood, he'd gone under the wheel?)

The following Thursday, as I was telling my prayer group about it, I said, "I know Seth's okay, but I just keep thinking about what *might* have happened." Jon Nelson, a prayerful man of great inner strength, stopped me. "Now wait a minute," he said. "You just stop thinking about what might have happened. It *didn't!* Be thankful instead!"

Did that ever bring me up short. Of course! That's the way to get out of negative thinking ruts. Give thanks for whatever there is of good in the situation. And there always *is* some good, if you look for it. A few days ago, I came across a footnote in my *Jerusalem Bible,* pertaining to Romans 3:24: "Gratitude to God is the fundamental and necessary disposition for grace." It is true. Gratitude was the hoist that got me out of the quicksand of my negative thoughts and back in touch with a peaceful spirit.

By Thinking of Positive Things

A recent item on National Public Radio brought out the fact that people who are depressed have a very hard time thinking about something positive in order to get their minds off the negative event or emotion. In depression they tend to get their minds off one negative by thinking about another negative! Perhaps they need Paul's encouragement to focus their thoughts on "whatever is true, whatever is honorable, whatever is just, whatever is pure, whatever is lovely, whatever is gracious, if there is any excellence, if there is anything worthy of praise, think about these things" (Philippians 4:8, RSV). That's very hard to do when you're depressed, and you probably won't do it unless you make an intentional decision about it. First acknowledge your pain to yourself, perhaps by telling your inner child that you are aware of her tears. Then deliberately write down just *one good thing* for each of the above categories. You may not want to, but do it anyway. Peace of mind, like happiness, really is a decision as well as a grace, and it grows out of stared-down pain.

By Trusting God's Motherly Love

There's something else that helps me to release my concerns to Him. It is this. In many places in the Bible, God's love is compared with that of a mother. It's very consoling to think that God's love is not only fatherly but also motherly. Listen to these words from Isaiah 66:12–13 (RSV), "As one whom his mother comforts, so I will comfort you."

And these: " 'Can a woman forget her sucking child, that she should have no compassion on the son of her womb?' Even these may forget, yet I will not forget you" (Isaiah 49:15, RSV).

God is not only our protector (a fatherly quality) but also our *nurturer* (a motherly trait). When I need power, I pray to Almighty God, but when I'm a hurt child, I like to think of the feminine qualities of a mothering God, who will comfort me, feed my spirit, give me rest, hold my problems for me for a while, or maybe even provide a warm lap for me to snuggle into, so that I can know I am safe and protected.

There are times when God has given me the gift of this kind of womblike love, from which I may emerge a new person, have my life renewed, draw creative energy for living. Psalm 22:9–10 (RSV) hints at this womblike love: "Yet thou art he who took me from the womb; thou didst keep me safe upon my mother's breasts. Upon thee was I cast from my birth, and since my mother bore me thou hast been my God."

Phyllis Trible, a Bible scholar and seminary professor, adds marvelous new dimensions to my concept of God's love, when she points out that in the Hebrew Scriptures, the word that means *womb* is the root of the word translated "compassion," "lovingkindness" (KJV) or "steadfast love" (RSV). She further shows that the word used to speak of *God's own* compassion is this same word that also means womb. God's love, then, is a womblike love, a mothering love![7] The voice of God speaks through the prophet Jeremiah:

> Is Ephraim my dear son? my darling child?
> For the more I speak of him,
>   the more I do remember him.
> Therefore, my womb trembles for him;
>   I will truly show motherly-compassion upon him.
>   *Jeremiah 31:20, Trible*[8]

When I think of mothering, I think of one who feeds her children. God does this for you and me in Scripture, if we'll allow ourselves time to inwardly digest the living truths that rise up from the pages of our Bibles. So many times, when I've felt lonely or sad, my Bible reading for the day is just what I've needed to hear for comfort and consolation. Like a mother who knows the needs of her child better than anyone else, the Holy Spirit knows all of my hungers, and has prepared just the meal that will most surely feed me.

The Spirit also feeds us with the spiritual food of the Holy Communion. If, before I receive the elements, I offer to Him all of the turmoil and chaos and sinfulness of my life, I can become an empty chalice, a vessel ready to be filled with *Christ Himself.* And I have learned that, *ultimately, all of my hungers are for Him.* He is the only one who can finally overcome my loneliness, love me unconditionally, forgive my sins, and make me whole again. I need to remember this when I feel let down by a human being. Because we are all flawed, every human relationship is also imperfect. When we sense the disappointment in that, let it remind us that there *is* One who is absolutely faithful forever, always on our side, and who never abandons or betrays us. Partaking of Holy Communion makes me know this in my spirit. Jesus walks away from that banquet table with me!

Worshiping with a community of believers is another way in which the Spirit feeds us, whether it's in a great cathedral among thousands, with glorious music and eloquent words, or in a quiet living room where two or three have gathered together to pray in halting syllables and everyday words. In either setting, the Holy Spirit may gather us under His wings, breathe on us the breath of Life, and transform us from the many into the one body of Christ.

But food for the spirit is not available only within the stained glass enclosures of church buildings, nor is it limited to those activities that are traditionally thought of as religious. The Holy Spirit spreads out a table for us so that we may feed on the beauty of nature, of music, of fine art, of drama, poetry, and story. All the aesthetic joys are food for the soul. When we're feeling empty, we can help ourselves to this heart-filling nourishment. Often, after an exhausting day, I go into the living room, turn on some quiet classical music, turn off the lights, and lie down on the couch, just letting the music soak into me. Sometimes I feel as though I'm floating away on the chords. Always it helps me to rediscover that lovely center in me that connects with all that is beyond my get-up-and-go-to-work days.

Like a mother, the Holy Spirit guards us tenderly, comforts the sorrowful, gives rest to the weary, and holds hands with the sick and the dying. In all of these ways, the Spirit *nurtures.* It's a mothering kind of love that perfectly complements the power of the Father and the divine humanity of the Son. Perhaps, when your spirit is in turmoil, you will remember that your God is a mothering God, and, in raising your hands toward that womblike love, you will find the priceless gift of a peaceful spirit.

By Learning to Say No

Jason, the hero of our opening parable, discovered the three secrets of a peaceful heart: to know that God is your only power; to face your pain head-on and see it through; and to surrender your heart so that peace can find you. There is a strange paradox in that surrender. It is this: in saying *yes* to God, you may have to say *no* to some of the human demands put on you. You will have to make some prayerful choices about what you will and will not do. Inability to do this is a powerful destroyer of peace of mind. How many times have you agreed to do something that you really didn't want to do, simply because you didn't feel you had the right to say no? Most of us have grown up lugging a heavy load of duty-consciousness. An honest sense of duty is a good thing, as long as we periodically examine it to be sure that it is realistic and valid for us. Maybe we should think about some of the ways we feel duty-bound.

It cannot be your duty to do anything that violates your own integrity. Of course, this means you aren't expected to do anything that you feel is wrong in God's eyes or your own. But it also includes most of those things you do that just don't fit with who you really are inside. God created the person I am. If I fail to be true to that, I lose my peace of mind.

At one time in my life, I got drawn into a social whirl. I was spending a large part of my time at bridge parties, luncheons, and clubs. My inner self was screaming because I didn't want to be away from my children that much and also because I'm an introvert and too much of that sort of thing leaves me drained. Yet, for quite a while, I felt unable to say no when the invitations came. Thanks be to God that I finally found the courage to get off of that merry-go-round! It was just not for me.

Learn to say no to those things that go against your nature. Of course, there are exceptions to this, especially in the workplace. In any career, there are certain things we have to do that don't fit our nature. We can put up with some of that if the overall picture is congruent with our abilities and interests. And of course, God sometimes calls us to try something that feels unnatural in order that we might grow. As in all of life, the rule is: submit it to God, listen, and then follow His leadings. I am sure that He won't lead you into anything that would violate your integrity.

It cannot be your duty to do something that would sacrifice your spiritual development. This can involve big things, such as career choices, as well as little, daily choices. For example, on busy mornings I sometimes make a choice between straightening the house and having my prayer time. I'm sure you can guess which one wins! However, there was a time when I'd have chosen the other way out of a sense of duty, thinking I didn't really have a right to put my spiritual growth ahead of daily tasks. If you find that you're too busy to give much time to your own spiritual growth, maybe you should see what "duties" you're putting ahead of it.

It cannot be your duty to give to every worthwhile cause. I think it's very important to deliberately decide where your giving will be. First, it's essential to give to the organization(s) from which you receive spiritual nourishment. For most of us, this means, primarily, our churches. Next, I think we need to choose one or more worthy causes that are dear to our hearts and support them as fully as we possibly can. Beyond that, whenever you're asked to donate to some cause, ask yourself if you want to scatter your resources or to focus them. Of course, we don't want to be rigid about this. If we see a need and sense that God wants us to respond by giving spontaneously, we need to be free to do that. But we shouldn't give out of guilt or out of a sense that we must save the world. We have to say no to some requests so that our yes to others will be more effective.

It cannot be your duty to take responsibility for the emotions or actions of other adults. I have a friend whose husband is a recovered alcoholic. She says that one of the first things she learned in Al-Anon (a support group for spouses of alcoholics) was to stop making herself responsible for her husband's behavior. When he missed work because of a hangover, for example, she was told to refuse to call in and make excuses for him. When his driver's license was revoked for thirty days for driving while intoxicated, she was to let him walk to work rather than "rescue" him by taxiing him around. "It was the hardest thing I ever did," she said, "but I see now that it was the most loving thing. Gradually, he began to take responsibility for his own actions, and that was the beginning of his recovery."

In the final tally, each of us is responsible not only for our own actions but also for our emotions. We really cannot protect other people from their own feelings. During a conference with the therapist who was treating my daughter for depression, I said that I had "bent over backward" to give Karen extra attention when her brother was born. "I tried really hard not to make her jealous," I said. The therapist explained to me that there is no way that a mother can protect her child from jealousy when a new baby enters the family. It's a normal emotion. So are anger, hurt feelings, frustration, and elation. They are part of the human condition. She helped me to see that, even as an adult, I cannot be responsible for anyone's feelings but my own. To try to "protect" another person from his or her feelings is likely to send that person into denial, which is an unhealthy state of mind. So if you're trying to protect someone from his/her own feelings, let yourself off the hook! It may be the most helpful thing you can do for them.

It cannot be your duty to suppress your feelings at the expense of your mental well-being. Swallowed feelings have a way of coming out. If they don't get expressed directly, they come out in little needling remarks, or self-loathing, or tension, or physical ailments—from headaches to arthritis, from heart attacks to cancer. Though you can't tell the boss off, you can wait till you get home and scream into a pillow or throw books onto the bed with a fury, or pull your dog up onto your lap, tell him the whole story, and cry out all of your self-pity. I've never known a dog who wasn't a sympathetic listener. My Oscar looks up at me with his big, sad, brown eyes and whines gently when I cry. Say no to lugging around emotional baggage. That's saying yes to peace of mind.

It cannot be your duty to give up your own God-given uniqueness in order to fit into someone else's mold. Bill is an outdoorsman. He loves to hunt and fish and camp out. His wife, Jackie, loves opera, ballet, and art exhibits. For the first several years of their marriage, each one thought the other had some serious character defect because they didn't "appreciate the finer things in life," and both were miserable a good part of the time. When they finally gave up on changing each other, Bill found a buddy who appreciated being outdoors as much as he did, and Jackie now goes with her sister to cultural events. The couple also found some things they both liked to do, such as playing Scrabble and viewing 1950s movies on their VCR. Say no to giving up your uniqueness.

It cannot be your duty to save the world. Only Christ can do that. He gives you portions of His work to do, but you can accomplish them only by His power.

I feel very certain that *God does not overload us.* Saying no has always been hard for me, but realizing that Jesus delegated some of the heavy responsibility of His ministry to others has helped to free me. Remember the words of Christ that formed the basis of chapter 8: "For my yoke is easy, and my burden is light" (Matthew 11:30). Unless we choose pleasing Christ as our number-one goal, we'll find ourselves saying yes to too many requests and not giving our best to any of them. So, "let your yes be yes and your no be no" (James 5:12, RSV).

If we can travel lightly through life, letting nothing become more important to us than God, He will go before us to "make the crooked places straight" and the rough ways smooth (Isaiah 45:2), and we shall truly have that "peace . . . which passes all understanding" (Philippians 4:7, RSV). The power of the Father, plus the courage of the Son, plus the nurturing of the Holy Spirit equals a peaceful spirit.

NOTES

1. William Shakespeare, cited in *The New Dictionary of Thoughts,* compiled by Tryon Edwards ([Bloomington, Ill.]: Standard Book Company, 1965), p. 458.

2. Mary Ruth Howes, in a letter to the author, February 8, 1989.

3. Martin Luther King, Jr., *The Words of Martin Luther King, Jr.,* selected by Coretta Scott King (New York: New Market Press, 1983), p. 24.

4. Charlotte Davis Kasl, *The Nature of Co-dependency* (New York: Houghton Mifflin, 1988), p. 3.

5. Paul Welter, *Connecting with a Friend* (Wheaton, Ill.: Tyndale House, 1985), p. 15.

6. Gordon Scott, "Help from Outside to Find Inner Peace," *Faith at Work* (January/February, 1988), p. 13.

7. Phyllis Trible, *God and the Rhetoric of Sexuality* (Philadelphia: Fortress Press, 1978), pp. 31–59.

8. *Ibid.,* p. 45.

CHAPTER 10

The Gift of Being Able to Serve

Let us have grace, whereby we may serve God acceptably with reverence and godly fear.

Hebrews 12:28

The gift of a peaceful spirit leads directly to another gift. As we've seen, peace is not a tenant who moves in, taking up permanent residence in our lives. It is a grace that must be invited back, again and again. But here's the marvel of it: every time that white-winged dove enters through our opened door, we are nourished, renewed, and then coaxed out of our comfortableness and *drawn back into the world* to live in more meaningful ways. Instead of saying, on the way out the door, "Thanks for your hospitality, but I've got to be going now," the Holy Spirit says, "Now that you are refreshed and renewed, come fly with me. I will be your wings in the world!"

This is, perhaps, the most *lasting* grace because, equipped with His wings, we may be able to serve in ways that we've never before dreamed we could. Now our lives can take on new meaning, a meaning that may continue to reverberate in the world long after our earthly life is past.

We Are Partners with God

We can never adequately serve God except by His grace. I have learned that as long as I think *I'm* doing the work, it falls short. Sure, there have been times when my work has been acceptable, even though I've plowed right through, forgetting to ask—and listen—for God's guidance. However (and I think this is a very important point), *the invisible effects of our serving are of far greater value than the visible ones.* What may appear successful by the world's standards will most certainly not serve its highest spiritual purpose unless God has been invited to participate in the process. And, conversely, a small, seemingly insignificant act performed *with* Him may be a pebble in the spiritual lake, sending out waves and waves and waves of grace, affecting lives of people we may never meet.

As We Offer Our Work to God

God can use even the most humdrum task, such as sweeping, filing, cleaning, typing, waiting tables, or stocking shelves, for *His* purposes. It is not so much a matter of outer results as of inner movement. Simply doing the nearest thing that needs to be done—the task at hand—with an awareness of God's presence elevates it to a form of prayer, and prayer changes lives.

Take sweeping the kitchen floor, for example. It may seem completely inconsequential. It'll just have to be done again tomorrow. But if you do it as an act of love for Christ, it will affect you—your mind, your emotions, and especially your spirit. That clean kitchen floor has a positive effect on your family, whether or not they consciously realize it, because God's invisible imprint is on it. Your attitude has also been stamped with God's love as you swept. And here's the thrilling part: *any task that is offered to God is transformed from physical substance to spiritual substance.* Think again of the spiritual dimension as a body of water, into which your act of loving service is cast. Visualize the rings of outward movement made by that pebble. Realize that an act of labor performed prayerfully and lovingly is transformed into spiritual energy to be used by God in His work of fulfilling the promise of Ephesians 1:10, that "he might gather together in one *all things* in Christ, both which are in heaven, and which are on earth; even in him" (italics mine).

Remember our Lord's parable about the talents? The servants who handled little things well proved that they could be used by God for greater purposes (Matthew 25:21). Here's something you might like to try. For one day, each time you begin a task (grocery shopping, examining a patient, waiting on a customer, or whatever work your day brings), offer it as a gift to Christ. Then close your eyes just long enough to picture a pebble being dropped into a quiet lake, and see the ripples moving out from it. If you decide to try this, don't get rigid about it. You will surely forget sometimes during the day, but I think if you sincerely try to offer each task to Him, you'll be richly, richly rewarded. A shift will take place within you, and your work will take on new meaning and value.

As We Trust God to Work in and with Us

The goal, then, is to keep God in our work, both spiritual and secular. There is a Scriptural affirmation that has helped me with this, and even though I've written about it elsewhere, I'd like to share it with you because it has virtually transformed my approach to serving. Several years ago, I spent an extended weekend in private retreat at the Crosier Retreat Center in Hastings, Nebraska. During that time, I asked God to make me ready to serve Him. One of the Bible readings given to me by my spiritual director was Job 23:1–14. In that passage, Job complains about not being able to find God. I saw myself in it, and maybe you will find yourself in Job's words, too.

"Behold, I go forward, but he is not there; and backward, but I cannot perceive Him: On the left hand, where he doth work, but I cannot behold him: he hideth himself on the right hand, that I cannot see him."

Yet, even though he can't feel God's presence, Job affirms that God is very much aware of him: "But he knoweth the way that I take . . . my foot hath held his steps, his way have I kept and not declined . . . I have esteemed the words of his mouth more than my necessary food."

Now comes the life-changing affirmation: *"He performeth the thing that is appointed for me"* (verse 14, italics mine). When I left the retreat center that Sunday afternoon in January, I had no idea that God was going to put me to work leading four prayer retreats in three different cities, all in the shortest month of the year! But I carried those words of Job in my heart. Every morning when I woke up, I affirmed that, since God gave me this work, He'd see it through with me. I said Job's affirmation over and over as I did my routine, daily things, such as brushing my teeth, cooking, washing the dishes, and I affirmed it every time I sat down to work on my speaking preparations, even though it sometimes seemed to me that God was leaving it all up to me. By the time the month was over, it was diamond-clear to me that God truly had performed my work *for* me by being in it *with* me. That has been confirmed for me again and again in the years since.

Maybe you'll decide to write Job's words on a card to place in your kitchen, on your desk, or someplace else that's near your work.

What Is Christian Service?

No matter what your work is, God wants to be in it with you. It's especially important to stay sharply aware of our partnership with God when we're about His business. What do you think of when you hear the term *Christian service?* Feeding the hungry? Giving your weekly tithe? Singing in the choir? Teaching a Sunday school class? Making hospital visits? Inviting a lonely stranger for Thanksgiving dinner? All of those things are very important and part of Christian service; but perhaps the greatest service we give others is passing on the light of Christ.

Sharing Our Faith Through Friendship

I don't know about you, but I get butterflies in my stomach when I hear the word *evangelism.* Usually, it means that someone is about to ask me to invite a friend to church, or make a home visit, or talk about Jesus to the unchurched. I'm very uncomfortable with all of that, afraid of seeming pious, pushy, or self-righteous. I'm going to suggest something that, at first hearing, may seem shocking. It is this. If you feel that way, *don't do it.* You may succeed only in increasing others' resistance to organized religion.

I learned this from Mel Goebel, a young man who is very active in prison ministry. Because of his efforts and those of others like him, many lives have been radically changed; many lost souls have found their way to Jesus Christ. Here is what he told me:

"Before we go to visit a prisoner, we spend time in prayer, asking the Holy Spirit to lead us, to take charge of our hearts and of the words we speak. *We do not go until we have a solid sense of His leading.* Once there, we never walk in and start quoting Bible verses, or telling the prisoners that Jesus can save them, or even that God loves them. No. We simply befriend them. We spend time with them individually, listening to their pain, letting them know that we care, that we can be relied upon, that we accept them just as they are. When it comes naturally, we share with them some of the pain of our own lives and talk about our personal weaknesses, letting them know that we are human beings together.

"Somehow, in this process of befriending, barriers are overcome and individuals may begin to feel, perhaps for the first time ever, that they are not alone in the world. Almost always, the subject of faith comes up, but it is they and not we who bring it up. When that occurs, we refrain from the natural urge to bombard them with the Good News. Instead, we simply answer their questions and, when we feel led, we share our own spiritual story. That's all."

Mel paused thoughtfully and then said, "No, there's one more thing. We *stay in the relationship.* This is absolutely vital. Many of these people have been abandoned time after time in their lives. They need to know that *we* are faithful, in order that they can trust that *God* is faithful. We are wonderfully rewarded to find that they begin to seek us out, wanting to know more about our faith, more about Jesus. Many of them develop an insatiable appetite for the spiritual nourishment that can be found in the Bible. And all of this just flows naturally, in response to *their* questions and needs and desires. It is never, never forced. We've also found that this is not a one-sided deal. We, too, are nourished by the friendship. Our own faith grows, as we begin to see that there truly is a child of God in every person."

I think this approach is excellent, not only for prison ministry but in all of our reaching out to others in the name of Christ. True, most of the evangelizing you and I are called to do is not in prisons. But is it so different? Aren't most of us turned off by people who are eager to tell us what to do, who think they have all the answers, who speak as if from a superior position? I think that we can avoid causing walls to go up, if we pray for the Holy Spirit to guide us. Jesus said to His disciples, "Do not be anxious how or what you are to answer or what you are to say; for the Holy Spirit will teach you in that very hour what you ought to say" (Luke 12:11–12, RSV). If we first spend time in prayer, let go of our own agenda, and then follow the leadings of the Holy Spirit, we'll sense when it's appropriate to ask if someone would like to join hands and pray with us, or when our own faith story would be helpful to another, or when one of Jesus' parables might help someone see a problem in a clearer light. We'll also sense when it's best simply to befriend and wait, as Jesus Himself so often did.

Being Together in Christ

When we think of serving, we aren't likely to consider that just being together in Christ is part of our work for Him in the world. If someone asks you the ways you serve, you may list being on the altar guild, or helping with the every-member canvass, or being a lay reader. But you might not be as likely to list worshiping on Sundays, participating in a prayer group or Bible study, going to "Fun Night" at the church, or being involved in a support group. The reason we don't think of these things as serving is because we're doing them for ourselves, because we want to, and we're getting something back. They feel more like being served than serving. Yet they are truly both.

Worship. In what way is worship actually service? For the answer to that, let's go to Paul's wonderful metaphor of the church as one body, with Christ as its head (1 Corinthians 12:12, Ephesians 4:15, Colossians 2:19). Paul makes it clear that the church is a body—that is, a living organism, animated by the Spirit. Like a human body, its very life on earth depends on its *unity,* its being together. Coming together in

Christ serves our Lord because it continues His earthly incarnation. And we serve each other when we meet as parts of His family for worship, because the touch of spirit upon spirit vitalizes our faith. By the grace of God, your spirit can reach out and become part of mine. This touch of your spirit on mine can empower me to do things and be things that I could never manage on my own.

Our coming together for worship serves God and one another in the same way the circulatory system serves the body. It keeps the life-force flowing. Being with others for worship is one of the most valuable—and certainly one of the most rewarding—parts of Christian service.

Last night I talked with a friend who is out of town visiting relatives. She told me that every morning since she's been there, her brother-in-law has had to jump-start her car. What an apt metaphor for the charge of spiritual energy that we give and receive when we meet together for worship.

Last Sunday was Mother's Day, and my children were all out of town. I felt very much alone and sad, sitting there in the pew by myself, watching other mothers coming in with their families. My spiritual energy was running on "Low," and I was choking back tears. Moments before the service started, I heard movements a few rows behind me and then felt the touch of a hand on my shoulder. It was my good friends Carolmae and Jim Petersen. Carolmae motioned for me to slide over, and they sat down with me. Suddenly I felt in the midst of family—loved, cared for, precious. I left the service feeling spiritually recharged. I hope there are times when I also charge the spiritual batteries of others, just by being near them and worshiping with them.

Prayer groups. Another way to serve is by belonging to an intercessory prayer group. But maybe you don't have time. I didn't think I did, either. When my friend Carolmae invited me to attend a small intercessory prayer group that was just starting, I thought I couldn't work it into my busy schedule. I decided to go once, though, to see what it was all about. I didn't realize, until I had been there several times, what a great, deep hunger I had been feeling for a long, long time—a spiritual loneliness that had been covered over and hidden by busyness.

I wonder how many people reading these words have an inner ache that they try to blot out, with work or frantic play, or social engagements, or some other numbing device. If you're vaguely aware of something like this, you may want to consider the possibility that it could be spiritual loneliness. Maybe finding or starting your own prayer group or Christian support group would help ease that dis-ease for you. Small group participation has certainly done that for me. Perhaps it's because our Lord promised that "where two or three are gathered together in my name, there am I in the midst of them" (Matthew 18:20).

Our little group meets for just an hour once a week. Usually, there are only five or six of us, although it is open to anyone. Over the past seven years, we have laughed together, cried together, and prayed together. It has been a home base from which to reach out to others who are in pain and to minister to each other. Something happens when we come together. The *bonding* we have helps us to know what it means to be one body in Christ (1 Corinthians 12:12).

Perhaps there are some small groups or weekday services at your church, too. Every weekday morning, our assistant priest and a small assortment of come-as-you-are parishioners sit together in silence in the chapel for ten or fifteen minutes, and then read the Scripture lessons for the day, closing with the Lord's Prayer. It takes only half an hour, but in that time of being present together in God's love, little and big hurts have been healed, lives have been graced, loads have been lightened. Some people drop in on their way to work; some (me, for example!) leave stacked dishes and unmade beds; some show up once or twice a month; some are there every day. It's just *open* and available. If you'd like to start your day this way and your church doesn't offer anything like it, maybe a talk with your pastor would get something going. If not, you might see if another local church has Morning Prayer. We are all Christians together. They'd welcome you, I'm sure, without expecting you to join their church. Perhaps you'll want to invite them to something at *your* church, too!

Meeting to Support One Another

There are support groups available now for just about every kind of problem, from alcoholism, to gambling, to overeating. But not all problems fit into categories. Several months ago, a couple of my friends started talking about the fact that they felt the need for a support group of some kind but they didn't fit into any of the "Anonymous" groups already established in our town. So they sat down and made a list of a few people they both knew they'd feel comfortable with and that they knew they could trust. After careful consideration, they approached a third lady. The three of them decided to ask me to join them. And that's how our little Monday noon Hesed group began. (*Hesed* is the Hebrew word that is used for God's faithful love.) We decided to limit our group to just the four of us because we're all busy and our time together is limited to just a long noon hour. This way, there's time for each one to talk about whatever has come up during the week that needs to be processed.

If you decide to start a Christian support group, here are a few simple things to keep in mind. Choose people that you trust and feel safe with, people you know well enough to be sure they won't try to monopolize things or control the group. Confidentiality must be an absolute hard-and-fast rule. The only things each member can talk about outside of the group are the things she herself said. No one should give advice to another, unless it is specifically asked for. No one should bring up another person's problems. In other words, it is not acceptable for someone else to ask you, "How did you and your son get along this week?" If *you* want to talk about that subject, you must bring it up.

A good way to begin is for each person to give her spiritual autobiography, beginning with early memories and ending with the present. It's a way of getting to know one another on a deeper level, which creates a close spiritual bondedness. Remember that this is not a social occasion. We meet in our homes, but it's understood that the hostess is not to do any extra cleaning, and each person brings a sack lunch, so that the focus stays on why we're there—to support each other in our pain, to share our joys, and to grow spiritually.

Of course, many people are unable to take a long lunch hour. Working people can meet in each other's homes in the evening, or get together on Sunday afternoons, or at whatever time is convenient for them. The guidelines given above could serve for these groups, too. Or, for excellent guidance on how to start and to lead an emotional and spiritual growth group, you may wish to write to: Yokefellows, Inc., Burlingame Counseling Center, 2435 El Camino Real, Millbrae, California 94030.

Serving Through Personal Prayer

We've been talking about serving by being together in Christ, but it's also important to remind ourselves that service through prayer is not limited to groups. Private intercessory prayer is also one of the highest and best ways to serve God. During the past few years, I have discovered some special ways to pray that have added extra dimensions to my prayers for others. From a man I talked to in the dentist's office, I learned to pray my way through the daily newspaper, asking help for those whose problems are in the headlines, as well as asking for guidance for each political leader or public figure who is mentioned. Though I don't do this every time I read the paper, when I do, I am blessed with a deep sense of the oneness I share with every other human being.

When we pray for others, the question always arises, "How do I know what to pray for? How can I be sure that my intercessions are God's will?" Those are very good questions. I believe we can't be absolutely sure—ever—that what we ask is God's will. But, we can conclude our intercessory prayer with a statement such as, "This, Lord, or something better," knowing that God understands each person's need and how those needs can best be met.

So why pray at all, since God already knows the need? The metaphor of the pebble in the lake opened to me an exciting answer to that question. The spiritual energy generated by prayer "move[s] upon the face of the waters" (Genesis 1:2—we're created in God's image, remember), and the invisible substance of the universe moves in response. We actually tap into the *spiritual substance from which every good thing proceeds.* (See Hebrews 11:1.) Our prayers, directed toward individual people and specific circumstances, break through barriers of time and space. Always, always, prayer has a *spiritual* effect on those for whom we pray, even if the physical situation doesn't change. More of God's spiritual energy is released into that person or circumstance. And in the process, into us as well. *We* are also changed. Isn't that a thrilling realization?

It's very important to realize that *intercessory prayer does not have to take form in words.* When I'm unsure about how to pray for a person, I simply quiet myself until I sense the inner presence of God. Sometimes He makes Himself known as a resplendent light behind the darkness of my closed eyes. Then I simply speak the person's name into that light, or visualize her or him surrounded by God's radiance. Even when I don't sense the light, even when I seem unable to feel the presence of God, I can simply affirm that He *is* present and quietly speak the person's name, sometimes again and again. That's enough. It is done. At other times I go, in my imagination, to a pleasant place where I've met Jesus in the past. Then I bring the other person into His presence in that setting and simply *stay there* for a while.

These forms of prayer may not seem like praying to you at first. We are so conditioned to think of prayer as saying words. It may be hard to simply wait with Jesus. Can't you hear Peter and James and John saying in Gethsemane, "A whole hour, Lord?" Yet this silent waiting bears great, rich gifts—gifts that fan out to other people, other places; gifts that can begin to change the world.

> *O God, help us to serve through prayer, both the familiar, word-bound kind and the lift-off kind, each bearing the imprint of the white-winged dove, messenger of Your grace.*   Amen.

Serving God in Our Careers

In addition to our specifically Christian service, our secular work can also be a way of serving God. This really begins when we decide to turn our will over to Him and let Him lead us into the career in which we can best serve Him. I'm convinced that the closer we come to using the talents and abilities we were born with, directed by the interests we develop along the way, the nearer we are to doing God's will in our work. By talents, I don't mean that you have to be a born musician, artist, or writer. Some have a talent for leadership, while others are truly talented followers. Some have talents for physical activity, while some are better suited to quiet, thinking work. Some need a succession of new experiences, while others prefer the familiarity of more repetitious work. I don't believe this is accidental. I think God created us with our unique capabilities and preferences. I'll go even further and say that I believe that, if it could ever happen that each person were doing work uniquely suited to his or her God-given spirit, our world would operate at its maximum potential.

Finding the Right Work

So how does one find that just-right work? I think it has to begin with prayer for guidance, followed by an offering of one's life to God to use according to His eternal plan. Then it's very important to *listen to your heart,* because God will give you feedback that will help you find your way (examples will follow). Probably the hardest part comes next: Learn to follow the nudgings of the Holy Spirit. So often, we pray for guidance, but when it comes, we don't have the courage to follow it! It's very possible, even likely, that you are meant to do one type of work at one time in your life and another later. Also, God's way of directing you to your best choice of career may be *by way of other work,* work that somehow makes you better able to serve in your special niche later. So, I'm not suggesting that you sit back and wait until the perfect job comes along. No. Begin with whatever is available that comes closest to being a "fit" for you. It may very well lead to something else, which in turn may be an opening into something else, which finally brings you to the work for which God created you.

This has been true in my life. I intended to become an actress but became a speech therapist instead. Then, after being a full-time mother for quite a few years, I went back to college, got a master's degree in English, and taught that subject on the college level for a number of years, during which I did some rather sporadic writing. Finally, I have become a full-time writer, and I sense that I've "come home." However, I know that the other things I did on the way here were not wasted. Each had its own value and, in fact, contributed to my ability to better serve God in my present capacity.

This movement by way of other work that creates unique capabilities sometimes happens in rather stunning ways. My good friends Jan and Eugene Ward call 1985 "the year of the miracles." As a young man, Eugene was a monk and later a priest at St. Meinrad Abbey, a Benedictine monastery in Indiana. In addition to serving as guest master for the Abbey, he also reconstructed the Abbey church organ. When Eugene was in his thirties, he attended an organists' convention and happened to sit next to a nice-looking young woman named Jan. These two kept in touch by mail, and after three years of prayerful consideration, Eugene decided to leave the monastery. Eventually, he and Jan were married and took up residence in Louisville, Kentucky. Although he continued his career as an organ builder, Eugene sometimes felt restless due to the fact that he'd had to give up his priesthood when he married.

In 1985, Eugene was hired by my home church to install and reconstruct their new organ. He later learned that, on the day he arrived, the rector's wife, Nancy Peek, had said to three or four people, "That man is not here just about the organ. Something else is going on." The project took a full year, and during that time, the parishioners came to consider Eugene as part of their church family. As his time in Kearney drew near the end, several different people, each unaware of the others' thoughts, asked him what he'd think about the possibility of becoming an Episcopal priest. The fact was that he and Jan *had* talked about that now and then over the years, but it had been all on a thinking level. The Spirit had not yet seemed to be in it.

One afternoon, Eugene was standing on a high scaffolding in the back of the church, installing organ pipes, when he heard the slow, shuffling footsteps of an elderly gentleman of the parish. When Dr. Westerfield said, "I think you should become an Episcopal priest and stay with us as our curate," Eugene experienced a sudden blinding flash. He describes it as "one of the most dramatic moments of my life." He immediately climbed down, went to the rector's office, and told Father Peek that he wanted to look into the possibility of becoming an Episcopal priest. Two days later, Father Peek asked him to become our pastoral minister. The Wards discussed the call with their children, and it was decided. The family has been a marvelous addition to our parish. On June 3, 1988, the priestly orders of Eugene L. Ward were officially recognized by the Episcopal Church.

Father Eugene serves in his own unique way. Having lived the monastic life for fourteen years, he creates a center of silence and peace within the church. Having been guest master, he knows how to make people feel welcome and cared for. His and Jan's musical talents have added new dimensions to our worship services. I had not known Eugene long before I realized that, for him, the highest form of prayer is *listening.* This has made it possible for God to prepare him for, and lead him into, his singular ministry.

I have told you about the Wards because I think there is a pattern in the way they have learned to follow God's leadings. If you feel you've not yet found your niche in God's plan, or that you might be ready for a change of career, here is a simple pattern for you to follow: Pray, Listen, Act, Yield. It's easy to remember because it's an acronym—P-L-A-Y. And isn't that what truly fulfilling work is? I have heard Father Eugene say, many times, "I just don't feel that what I'm doing is work. I'm just doing what I most enjoy and getting paid for it!" Isn't that what we'd *all* like to be able to say? Perhaps if we use the "PLAY" way of prayerfully letting God's plan for us unfold, we'll be able to say that, too.

Finding the Creative Edge

It seems to me that no matter what our work is, a *creative dimension* may be added to it. We are, after all, made in the image of the One who said, "Let there be . . ." and suddenly there was. I believe that God calls you and me to be co-creators with Him in His ongoing act of creation, whether it's by tastily putting together whatever happens to be in the pantry; by finding a way to farm that corner of the field that isn't reached by the irrigation system; or by thinking up a way to make office reports more interesting to prepare.

Earlier in the chapter, we talked about offering each new task as a gift to Christ, and visualizing the ripples moving out from the pebbles dropped in the water of the spiritual substance. That's one way to find the creative edge in your daily work. Here are some related ideas. Choose the ones that best seem to fit you and the way you work.

A few years ago, I talked with a lady who put little plastic toys in boxes of caramel corn as the packages passed by her on a conveyor belt. Now that's a boring, repetitious job, no matter how you view it. How could creativity enter into it? One day, the woman asked God to help her get through another tedious day. A few minutes later, a thought came to her. After that, every time she put a toy in a box, she said a little greeting she'd read in the Bible: "Grace be unto you, and peace, from God" (1 Corinthians 1:3). She told me that, as she prayed this way for the children who would find the surprises, her whole attitude toward her work changed. I have no doubt that the children who received those toys were also blessed by the woman's creative use of her time and work. Her prayers were pebbles cast into the spiritual substance, and I am sure that the ripples from them have spread in all directions. She may never know the effects of her creativity, but the grace of her prayers continues unbounded.

The key to being more creative in your own work is to realize that *creativity is already within you.* Since you were created in God's image, you *are* a creative being. You need only to get yourself out of the way. Creativity is truly a form of spirituality. If you're looking for a creative solution to a specific problem, for example, after you've researched it and thought about it and worked on it until you can't stand it anymore, *let go of it completely.* You may be surprised to find that getting your self-conscious self out of the way releases the exhilarating creative energy of the One who spoke the universe into being.

Another way of letting go is to balance mental work with physical tasks in order to stay fresh. This may require some shifting of mental gears, but in the process you gain momentum that will carry you farther than a nose-to-the-grindstone approach.

Finally, if you're feeling overwhelmed, divide up the tasks into manageable, bite-sized segments. Let go of all but one thing, focusing on just that one segment, until it's done. This will free your mind and improve your ability to accomplish your goals.

Letting go also helps us claim the life-enriching gift of *satisfaction* in our work. A key factor is to get free of excessive attachment to the results of our labors. This has been a hard one for me, but when I'm able to do it, I get a taste of the gift, and it is worth savoring! Sometimes, after a long day's work, I'm not at all satisfied with what I've produced. But if I can offer it to God, flawed as it is, I find that in emptying myself, I've made room for His filling. Sometimes the missing ingredient presents itself the next morning (pure grace!); but even when it doesn't, I sense the gift of a deep satisfaction born of trusting Him. If you can offer each day's work to God, do the very best you can without getting too rigid and perfectionistic, and then completely release the results to Him, your work will be a source of profound contentment. It's all God ever asks of you. Having done that, you have fulfilled your mission for the day. Let it go. It's in God's hands. The waters are moving.

"You Will Go Out in Joy"

This singlemindedness is a very old key to serving, as old as the One who said, "Martha, Martha, you are anxious and troubled about many things; *one thing is needful.* Mary has chosen the good portion, which shall not be taken away from her" (Luke 10:41–42, RSV, italics mine).

And what is the one thing that is needful in order that we might claim every good thing? To gaze lovingly into the eyes of Jesus Christ; for it is there that we'll genuinely come to know that the gift of God's grace is *already ours,* and that within that grace every good gift waits. When we have come to know the joy of serving others, we'll begin to know a great secret: that God Himself is our truest, deepest, and most lasting joy. Let today be the day of your fresh start.

This morning, as I sit in my home office looking out over the greening valley behind the house, a vision for you is forming in my mind. I see a new greening of your life, as you begin to live in harmony with your inner truth by claiming the gift of being real.

I envision for you a leafing out of your intimacy with God, with yourself, and with other people. Like sky-reaching branches, I claim for you breakthrough thoughts, as you reach for the gift of expanding ideas. My vision for you includes a harvest of treasures, both earthly and heavenly, discerned, claimed, and accepted in love; and I see that you are yoked to the One who bears you up, lightens your load, walks beside you all the way.

In the heart of the little valley beyond my window is Kearney Lake. On this calm, windless day in early spring, the water is like a mirror. May that gentle picture be a reflection of your growing peacefulness of spirit; and may the claiming of all these gifts so fill you and feed you that you will be empowered to serve in a truly grace-filled way.

Come! Let us soar together on the wings of the Spirit!

For you shall go out in joy,
   and be led forth in peace;
the mountains and the hills before you
   shall break forth into singing,
    and all the trees of the field shall clap their hands.
                     —Isaiah 55:12 (RSV)

Amen.

Appendix One

In chapter 1, I told you that when I looked up the Scripture passages that tell about God's grace, I began to see that every truly worthwhile thing I've ever wanted is a gift of grace. Here are the references I promised you:

Grace makes it possible for us to have faith (Acts 18:28).

Gifts of the Spirit listed by Paul in 1 Corinthians 12:8–10: wisdom, knowledge, faith, healing, working of miracles, prophecy, discerning of spirits, speaking in various tongues, and interpretations of tongues.

Grace also brings:

salvation (Ephesians 2:5, 8);
wisdom and perception (Proverbs 4:7)
the ability to reach out to others (Acts 28)
power (Acts 20:33)
comfort and hope (2 Thessalonians 2:16)
strength (2 Timothy 2:1)
humility (James 4:6)
growth (2 Peter 3:18)
sufficiency (2 Corinthians 12:9)
cheer and respite (Ezra 9:8)
love and forgiveness (Luke 15:6–32).

It is only by grace that we are:

justified (Romans 3:24)
made righteous (Romans 5:17)
given eternal life (Romans 5:21)

Appendix Two

Here are a few selected Biblical affirmations that, if repeated frequently, can have a transforming effect on your life. Choose several that seem most powerful to you, or that are especially appropriate for your life situations. You might want to write or type those and place them around the house or workplace, where you'll see them often.

"This is the day which the Lord hath made. [I] will rejoice and be glad in it" (Psalm 118:24).

"Let not your heart be troubled, neither let it be afraid" (John 14:27).

"The things which are impossible with men are possible with God" (Luke 18:27).

"If God be for us, who can be against us?" (Romans 8:31)

"Thou shalt guide me with thy counsel" (Psalm 73:24).

"This is the refreshing" (Isaiah 28:12).

"God is our refuge and strength, a very present help in trouble" (Psalm 46:1).

"I have learned, in whatsoever state I am, therewith to be content" (Philippians 4:11).

"Be ye transformed by the renewing of your mind" (Romans 12:2).

"This one thing I do" (Philippians 3:13).

"I can do all things through Christ which strengtheneth me" (Philippians 4:13).

"Thou wilt keep him in perfect peace, whose mind is stayed on thee" (Isaiah 26:3).

"They that wait upon the Lord shall renew their strength" (Isaiah 40:31).

"Cast thy burden upon the Lord, and he shall sustain thee" (Psalm 55:22).

A NOTE TO THE READER

This original Guideposts book is brought to you by the same editors who prepare *Guideposts,* a monthly magazine filled with true stories of people's adventures in faith.

If you have found inspiration in this book, we think you'll find monthly help and inspiration in the exciting stories that appear in our magazine.

Guideposts is not sold on the newsstand. It's available by subscription only. And subscribing is easy. All you have to do is write Guideposts Associates, Inc., Carmel, New York 10512. For those with special reading needs, *Guideposts* is published in Big Print, Braille, and Talking Magazine.

When you subscribe, each month you can count on receiving exciting new evidence of God's presence and His abiding love for His people.